Party food

Trish Deseine

Party food

photography by Marie-Pierre Morel

HACHETTE illustrated

Digest this first!

Let's make one thing clear: this book is not for Ambassadors or DIY enthusiasts.

Ambassadors give sparkling soirées, arranged entirely by telephone. Such entertainments feature ice sculptures, pyramids of champagne, designer canapés, caterers who knock up delicious little dishes on the spot, all the while discreetly filling your glass. It's marvellous. Get yourself invited.

The DIYs, on the other hand, have done it all themselves. They've tipped out packets of peanuts and crisps onto paper plates with their own hands. They've spread 342 cold blinis with taramasalata and 433 slices of toast with rillettes garnished with gherkins. They've heated cans of cocktail sausages at the beginning of the evening, then leave them cooling on the sideboard, next to the dried-out mustard and the delicious dessert brought by the guests.

You've guessed it. Homemade feasts are not about mediocrity. Nothing to do with dinners or lunches organized at the last minute to fit in with the pressures of your life. A party should be anticipated, planned, thought-through, prepared – or it's not a party.

The ten rules of a well-planned party

Relax. The effort required is more to do with brainpower than brawn. Forget sophistication and difficulty. Go for simplicity and, as far as possible, for quality ingredients. Follow these ten rules (I've left out some obvious ones like warning the neighbours, setting aside somewhere for the coats, making coffee in presentable vacuum jugs, etc), let yourself be inspired by the recipes and themes of this book and all will go well.

1 You're not Marco Pierre White or Gordon Ramsay.

At this party you are not going to use caterers. So whatever you do, don't copy their presentations. This applies for dinners and lunches as well – don't try to recreate professional catering. If you want to try a chef's cooking, go to his restaurant. If you want magnificent and identical appetizers, buy them in.

Get some ideas from the professionals then do it your way, simply but with imagination, using the best ingredients you can afford.

As for the drinks, try to coordinate the alcohol. A decent wine that you have discovered and bought in quantity will go down better throughout the evening than an assortment from guests. This will avoid hangovers and the spoiling of good wines by them being served at the wrong temperature or at the wrong moment.

2 Think like an interior designer.

Remember the best parties when you were young? Guests squashed like sardines in half-darkness, glasses constantly refilled and music in the background, forced to make conversation, obliged to dance, incapable of not having fun.

If you want a sparkling ambiance, don't let your guests disperse and don't site the dance floor in a remote corner of the house. In any case, around midnight everyone will gather in the kitchen. So think carefully where to locate the buffet. Nothing dampens the atmosphere more than guests waiting their turn in a canteen-like queue. If you have more than 25, it's better to plan for two buffet tables with identical dishes, china, cutlery, glasses and decoration.

3 China, cutlery, glasses: make sure you have plenty.

Sale shops are overflowing with white china. You can get crockery at very reasonable prices. Go for medium plates and shallow bowls that can be used for salad, dessert or soup.

When I have more than 40 guests, I hire china and glasses. White or plain ones cost less. What's more, you can put them back into their boxes immediately they've been used, hidden under the buffet tablecloth. Not having to do the washing up is the real height of decadence. You just simply return them!

4 If you have 25 guests or more, get help.

Essential, if you want to enjoy your own party. I've often turned my babysitters into impeccable waitresses, thanks to an apron and a good briefing. Compared with my four wild kids, dealing with 60 lit-up guests is a piece of cake!

5 Don't improvise the music.

Overheated audio systems, amateur DJ dictators with a passion for Fleetwood Mac – it is *very* difficult to please everyone and to kit yourself out appropriately.

It's easy to keep 20 good friends grooving for an hour or two with a few CDs of everyone's favourites and a good hi-fi system, so that you don't find yourself exhausted by the end of the evening.

But if it's a party where the generations are mixed (a wedding or an engagement, for example) and you want all night dancing for 50 guests, it's essential to find a good DJ from a reliable disco or recommended from another party.

It's a real skill. DJs know how to read the mood at every moment and to adjust their playlist. They have great material and they love doing it.

6 For children? There's always a solution!

Ten year-olds and under

If you plan a party for this age group, have babysitters to watch the little ones, a suitable menu and a place where they can rest, watch a video, or sleep later on.

But having young children at a party for adults is strongly discouraged. I've tried it. Imagine a 12-month-old baby passed around the guest like a plate of sandwiches until 9.30: there's nothing like it to ruin the mood, make stains and translate your femme fatale image into that of a mother hen.

Other examples: thanks to big brothers, we twice came within a hair's breadth of a house fire. The first time it was through cocoa spilled over Hubert's tape deck and portable (sorry, Huby) and the second time it was caused by obsessive relighting of the adorable candles set at floor level.

If your children are like mine, once they're asleep not even *Dancing Queen* bawled in a hundred-decibel chorus by all the guests just below their room will wake them. The problem is to get them asleep BEFORE the guests arrive.

Try to distribute several of the tribe around other guests and provide a seasoned babysitter to leave them free to party themselves.

Teenagers

They can be a problem. There are two scenarios: either they make you feel like old wrinkly has-beens by sniggering in a corner, howling with laughter at the sight of your guests rocking to their Eminem CD, or you're the sort of parents who manage to override their adolescents' angst and press them into service as DJs. Either way, don't oblige them to attend.

7 Groups of friends.

We all have different groups of friends. To get them talking to each other, try a themed party (avoid *Barbie & Ken* before June because of the need for a suntan, *Ben Hur* or *The Man in the Iron Mask* because of the hire costs) or an easy quiz theme: 'What am I?' with clues given to everyone can go down well. But beware, some people may take it amiss to find themselves classified as 'mad cow' (*sorry*, Sophie).

Don't worry too much about making people mingle – they will do it of their own accord, eventually, if the ambience is right.

Older people

I don't share the ageism of certain adolescents, as mentioned in the preceding paragraph. My friends aged 60 and upwards have all of life's experience to impart, another freer life ahead of them and nothing to prove. Those who come to my parties enjoy mixing and chatting with everyone and are the last to leave the dance floor. Over to you.

8 Appetite comes with eating, thirst with drinking.

Think about the feeding timetable

There's always a critical moment, after the first or second glass, when the appetite of your guests revives like that of the giant in *Jack and the Beanstalk*.

To start with you'll have provided little canapés, dips or other DIY nibbles. But when the Great Hunger strikes, serve a soup, or a substantial sandwich, then carry on with the canapés before bringing on a 'main' dish.

It's very important that glasses can be refilled easily. Always ensure that guests can get to the drinks and delegate one or two friends to make the rounds with a bottle of champagne or mineral water.

9 Calculate the quantities.

Very, very difficult. I have no tips to impart. Even when I have followed expert advice, I always make twice as much of the food that is left and half as much of that which is scoffed immediately.

Another terribly unfair point: even if the food is divine, if there isn't enough your guests will remember only that they were left feeling hungry.

10 Serve food that's easy to eat.

Go for finger food or fork food.

For a buffet party, avoid everything that runs, drips, disintegrates in the hand or needs knife and fork and a more solid support than a pair of knees. Instead, take advantage of the wide range of breads (baguettes, ciabatta, focaccia, sourdough) to be found in the supermarket.

That vital spark

That's the end of my planning advice. On to the recipes.

All of this, however, is simply the décor and the accessories for the festivity. The most important ingredient is the actors: you and your guests.

You cannot manufacture atmosphere, the sparkle that will turn your party into a wonderful evening to be talked about for years. This magic is a rare and precious ingredient for which, unfortunately, I don't have the recipe.

Parties for paupers

We all know the feeling: we're so thrilled with our new home that we simply have to throw a party to celebrate.

But every last penny has gone on the mortgage or the deposit. How to do it well and cheaply?

Firstly, a BYO (bring your own) is required. Careful, this should not be the regulation PBAB (please bring a bottle) of teenage parties. A BYO should take the form of a bottle of champagne per head, elegantly suggested on the invitation card with a stylish addition 'bubbles appreciated' or 'BYOB' (bring your own bubbles).

This will reduce costs, avoid the hangovers caused by a mix of wine and assorted spirits and ensure a real party atmosphere all evening. All the same, make sure to keep two bottles chilled to await the arrival of other guests.

The food should be very simple, seasonal, and based around bread, pasta, fruit and vegetables. It's worth searching out good bread and going to your local market for all the other products. The more an ingredient is in season, the better and cheaper it will be. Take advantage of this.

Tomato and chilli

Makes a small bowlful
Preparation time: 3 minutes

250 g (8 oz) peeled canned tomatoes,
drained and lightly chopped
2 tablespoons olive oil
1 teaspoon chilli sauce (optional)
sea salt and freshly ground pepper

Mix all the ingredients and add the chilli sauce if you like
things hot!

Avocado, tomato, mascarpone and lime

Makes a small bowlful
Preparation time: 10 minutes

1 tomato, peeled
2 avocados, peeled
2 tablespoons mascarpone cheese
juice of 2 limes
salt and pepper

Mash the avocados and mix with the other ingredients.
Season to taste.

Feta and red pepper

Makes a small bowlful
Preparation time: 15 minutes

250 g (8 oz) Greek feta cheese, crumbled
1 red pepper, diced
100 ml (3^1/$_2$ fl oz) whipping cream
sea salt and pepper

Mix the ingredients with a fork until they reach a smooth
consistency.

Hummus and pine nuts

Makes a small bowlful
Preparation time: 15 minutes
Cooking time: 15 minutes

1 x 425 g (14 oz) can of cooked chickpeas,
drained and rinsed
3–4 tablespoons olive oil
8 tablespoons lemon juice
2 tablespoons tahini
4–5 tablespoons pine nuts, grilled
salt and pepper

Blend the chickpeas in a liquidizer with the olive oil, lemon
juice (to taste), tahini and half the pine nuts. Season.
Serve in a bowl, for dipping or spreading, decorated with
the rest of the pine nuts.

Grilled brioche, chicken liver pâté with port and juniper berries

Serves 6
Preparation time: 10 minutes
Cooking time: 15 minutes

4 tablespoons olive oil
1 shallot, chopped
250 g (8 oz) chicken livers
2 tablespoons port
5 juniper berries, crushed
6 slices of brioche, toasted
flat leaf parsley, chives (snipped), or chutney
sea salt, pepper

Heat 2 tablespoons of olive oil in a pan. Cook the shallot gently then add the chicken livers. When they are well done on the outside but still pink inside, deglaze the pan with the port. Remove the livers and process finely with the cooking liquid and the juniper berries. Season, adding olive oil if the mixture is too dry.
Spread on the toasted brioche slices and garnish with flat leaf parsley, chives, or chutney.

Garlic bread

Serves 6
Preparation time: 5 minutes
Cooking time: 10 minutes

150 g (5 oz) butter, softened
2 garlic cloves, crushed
1 tablespoon parsley, finely chopped
pepper
1 baguette

Blend together the butter, garlic and parsley, season with the pepper. Slice the baguette lengthways without cutting right through. Spread with the garlic butter, close up and cook at 180°C (350°F) gas mark 4 for around 10 minutes. Slice and serve.

Crostini with red onion jam and goats' cheese

Serves 6–8
Preparation time: 10 minutes
Cooking time: 1 hour

75 g (3 oz) raisins
olive oil
500 g (1 lb) red onions, finely sliced
75 g (3 oz) sugar
150 ml (¼ pint) red wine
2 tablespoons balsamic vinegar
1 tablespoon crème de cassis
2 thin French bread sticks (ficelles)
3 fresh goat's cheeses

Steep the raisins in hot water for around 30 minutes. Drain and set aside.
Heat 2–3 tablespoons oil in a pan. Cook the onions over a low heat for 10–15 minutes until golden.
Add the sugar, lower the heat and continue cooking for 10 minutes, until the onions are well softened and caramelized.
Add the raisins, wine, vinegar and crème de cassis and cook for 25–30 minutes until all the liquid is absorbed. Season and leave to cool.
Heat the oven to 180°C (350°F) gas mark 4.
Slice the bread into rounds and place on an ovenproof plate, adding a few drops of oil to each slice.
Bake for 4–5 minutes. Cool before spreading with the onion jam. Top each slice with a nugget of goat's cheese.

Almond croûtons

Makes 48 croûtons
Preparation time: 15 minutes
Cooking time: 5 minutes

75 g (3 oz) chopped almonds
1 teaspoon sea salt
12 slices white sandwich bread, crusts removed
150 g (5 oz) butter, melted

Preheat the oven to 200°C (400°F) gas mark 6.
Mix together the almonds and the salt. Dip each side of the bread in melted butter, then into the almonds.
Put on greaseproof paper or a silicone mat in an ovenproof dish and bake until golden (around 5 minutes).
Remove from the oven and cool on a rack.

Angel-hair frittata with bacon and cheese

Makes 25 pieces
Preparation time: 15 minutes
Cooking time: 5 minutes

200 g (7oz) streaky bacon, cut into strips
6 eggs
4 tablespoons crème fraîche
2 tablespoons chives, chopped
100 g (3$\frac{1}{2}$ oz) Parmesan, grated
250 g (8 oz) angel hair pasta, cooked according to packet instructions
butter, for frying

Lightly brown the bacon in a frying pan, drain on kitchen paper and set aside.
Beat the eggs with the crème fraîche and season lightly.
Add the chives, Parmesan and bacon and stir into the pasta.
Melt a knob of butter in a pan and pour in the mixture.
Cook very gently until the eggs begin to set and the top is golden. Turn and cook the underside. Remove from the pan and slice into wedges.
Serve warm or cold.

Note • To help turn the frittata, first slide it onto a plate and cover with another plate. Turn over and slide the frittata back into the pan.

Tartlets with tongue, capers and croûtons

Serves: 6
Preparation time: 10 minutes
Cooking time: 5 minutes for the croûtons

$\frac{1}{2}$ baguette
1 garlic clove, peeled
olive oil
2–3 slices ox tongue, from the deli counter
2 tablespoons capers
1 tablespoon parsley, chopped
6 small pastry shells
salt and pepper

Preheat the oven to 180°C (350°F) gas mark 4.
To make the croutons: rub the baguette with the garlic clove, then cut it into small dice. Sprinkle over a little olive oil and spread over a non-stick baking tray. Bake for 5 minutes until golden brown. Leave to cool.
Finely chop the ox tongue, mix with the capers, croûtons, parsley, salt and pepper, adding a little olive oil.
Put a spoonful in each pastry case and serve.

Tartlets of chopped beef cheek

Beef cheek is ideal for this recipe as it cooks down beautifully with long, slow cooking but if you can't find any, use minced beef and make up like little cottage pies sitting in the pastry shells.

Makes 18 tartlets
Preparation time: 30 minutes
Cooking time: 3 hours

2 tablespoons olive oil
1.5 kg (3 lb) beef cheek
3 carrots, diced
2 celery sticks, sliced
thyme, bay leaf
1 bottle wine
1 onion, studded with 2 cloves
7–8 large potatoes, peeled
150 ml ($\frac{1}{4}$ pint) whipping cream
30 g (1 oz) salted butter
HP or Worcestershire sauce, or mustard
18 pastry shells
100 g (4 oz) Gruyere cheese, grated
salt and pepper

Heat the oil in a cast-iron saucepan and lightly brown the beef all over. Add the vegetables and herbs and cook a few minutes longer. Add the wine, onion and a little salt and pepper (not too much, as the liquid will reduce a lot).
Cover and cook over a low heat for at least 3 hours.
Add water if necessary to prevent it drying.
Boil the potatoes until well-cooked then mash or purée them with the cream, butter and seasoning.
Dice the meat, season with salt, pepper and HP sauce.
Place a little meat in each pastry shell, cover with potato purée and sprinkle with Gruyere.
Reheat in the oven at 180°C (350°F) gas mark 4 for 5 minutes before serving.

Mini bouchées à la reine – almost

This is a little twist to the traditional filling for vol au vents.

Makes 18 mini vol au vents
Preparation time: 20 minutes

50 g (2 oz) unsalted butter
2 tablespoons flour
750 ml (1$\frac{1}{4}$ pints) chicken stock
5 boneless, skinless chicken breasts, lightly poached and diced
150 g (5 oz) button mushrooms, finely sliced
100 ml (3$\frac{1}{2}$ fl oz) crème fraîche
sea salt and pepper
18 small flaky pastry vol au vent cases

Melt the butter in a saucepan, add the flour and cook gently for several minutes, stirring all the while. Pour in the chicken stock and bring to the boil. Add the chicken and mushrooms and cook for a further 10 minutes. Add the crème fraîche, season to taste and fill the vol au vent cases (preheated for 5 minutes). The sauce can be prepared in advance, in which case reheat the bouchées gently for 5 minutes and fill just before serving.

Haricot beans with garlic and Parmesan rind

Serves 6–8
Preparation time: 10 minutes
Cooking time: 25 minutes

20 g ($^3/_4$ oz) butter
1 tablespoon olive oil
2 garlic cloves, finely chopped
2 shallots, finely chopped
1 x 400 g (13 oz) can haricot beans, drained and rinsed,
or 200 g (7 oz) dried haricot beans soaked overnight then rinsed and boiled for 30 minutes or until just soft, not mushy.
1 litre (1$^3/_4$ pints) chicken or vegetable stock
50 g (2 oz) Parmesan rind

Melt the butter in the oil then add the garlic and shallots and sweat for a few minutes. Add all the other ingredients, bring to the boil and cook for 20–25 minutes.
Remove the Parmesan rind, blend the soup in a liquidizer and season.
Serve, or set aside and reheat gently when ready to serve.

Spinach and potato

Serves 8
Preparation time: 10 minutes
Cooking time: 30 minutes

2 tablespoons olive oil
1 onion, finely chopped
handful of flat leaf parsley, chopped
1 litre (1$^3/_4$ pints) hot vegetable stock
2 waxy potatoes, sliced
500 g (1 lb) fresh spinach
2 Granny Smith apples

Heat the oil in a pan and sweat the onion without browning.
Add the parsley and cook for 1 minute, then add the hot stock and the potatoes and cook for 10 minutes.
Add the spinach and cook for a further 15 minutes.
Blend in a liquidizer.
Reheat the soup and pour into bowls. Top with the grated apples before serving.

Leek and orange

Serves 8
Preparation time: 10 minutes
Cooking time: 30 minutes

2 tablespoons olive oil
2 onions, finely chopped
2 celery sticks, chopped
750 g (1$^1/_2$ lb) leeks, white part, chopped
1 litre (1$^3/_4$ pints) vegetable or chicken stock
See page 38 (Cream of petit pois) for a quick stock recipe
whipping cream
juice and grated rind of 1 orange, or the pared zest

In a saucepan heat the oil and let the vegetables colour without browning. Add the stock and cook for around 20 minutes until the vegetables are soft. Blend in a liquidizer then stir in the cream followed by the orange juice and grated rind. This will make the soup deliciously creamy.

Garlic and almond cream

Serves 8
Preparation time: 10 minutes
Cooking time: 30 minutes

10 garlic cloves
6 slices country bread, crusts removed
300 ml ($^1/_2$ pint) milk
300 g (10 oz) almonds, blanched and ground
500 ml (17 fl oz) water (approximately)
salt and pepper

Preheat the oven to 190°C (375°F) gas mark 5 and roast the unpeeled garlic cloves for 25 minutes. When cool, squeeze out the pulp.
Soak the bread in the milk for a few minutes. Add the garlic pulp and the almonds and enough water to obtain a creamy consistency. Season to taste.
Serve chilled, or reheat gently before serving with a few drops of olive oil and croûtons made with buttered country bread.

Roast vegetables with basil and olive oil

Pecorino, lemon, crème fraîche

Roast vegetables with basil and olive oil

Serves 6
Preparation time: 10 minutes
Cooking time: 35 minutes

1 aubergine
1 courgette
2 tomatoes
1 onion
1 red pepper
4 tablespoons olive oil
2–3 tablespoons fresh basil
salt and pepper

Preheat the oven to 180°C (350°F) gas mark 4.
Cut the vegetables into chunks. Place in an ovenproof dish and pour the olive oil over. Roast for around 35 minutes. Season and stir into pasta. Sprinkle with basil.

Pecorino, lemon, crème fraîche

Serves 6
Preparation time: 10 minutes

175 g (6 oz) pecorino cheese, grated
grated rind of 2 lemons
350 ml (12 fl oz) whipping cream
salt and pepper

Mix the cheese with the grated lemon rind and cream.
Heat gently, season to taste and pour over pasta.

Broccoli, pine nuts, mascarpone

Serves 6
Preparation time: 5 minutes
Cooking time: 15 minutes

200 g (7 oz) pine nuts
2 heads fresh broccoli
280 g (8 oz) tub mascarpone
salt and pepper

Grill or dry-fry the pine nuts and set to one side.
Steam or boil the broccoli, then break into florets.
Stir into pasta with half the pine nuts and the mascarpone.
Garnish with the remaining pine nuts and serve immediately.

A good tomato sauce

Serves 6
Preparation time: 15 minutes
Cooking time: 25 minutes

1 tablespoon olive oil
1 garlic clove, crushed
500 g (1 lb) well-ripened tomatoes or 700–800 g ($1^1/_2$ –$1^3/_4$ lb) tinned tomatoes, deseeded and roughly chopped
1 tablespoon parsley, chopped
1 tablespoon basil, chopped
1 teaspoon sugar
1 teaspoon concentrated tomato purée
2 tablespoons red wine
Parmesan or pecorino cheese
salt and black pepper

Heat the oil in a pan and cook the garlic briefly, add the tomatoes, herbs and sugar. Simmer for 10 minutes then add the tomato concentrate and the wine. Cook for a further 15 minutes. Season to taste and serve with pasta, or a roast, and a bowl of freshly grated Parmesan or pecorino for diners to help themselves.

Tip • Make 'homemade' tomato concentrate by mixing sun-dried tomatoes into pasta.

Broccoli, pine nuts, mascarpone

Baked apples with cinnamon butter and demerara sugar

Serves 6
Preparation time: 10 minutes
Cooking time: 30 minutes

6 cooking apples
175 g (6 oz) butter, softened
1 tablespoon cinnamon
3 tablespoons Demerara sugar

To serve:
mascarpone
seeds from 1 vanilla pod

Preheat the oven to 180°C (350°F) gas mark 4.
Core the apples, but not quite through or the filling will leak out. Run the point of a sharp knife round each apple to prevent it bursting while cooking. Mix the butter with the cinnamon and sugar. Fill the apples with the spicy butter mixture and bake for around 30 minutes. Serve hot with vanilla mascarpone (mix the seeds from a vanilla pod into 4–5 tablespoons mascarpone).

Ice cream with breadcrumbs and caramel sauce

Serves 10
Preparation time: 15 minutes

1 litre (1³/₄ pints) good vanilla ice cream
4 slices white sandwich bread, crusts removed

Remove the ice cream from the freezer to soften. Toast the bread lightly and leave to cool. Using a food processor or your fingers, crumble the bread finely and mix into the ice cream. Return to the freezer until firm. Serve with caramel or fudge sauce.

French bread pudding

Serves 6
Preparation time: 10 minutes
Resting time: 20 minutes
Cooking time: 40 minutes

6 or 7 slices of day-old white sandwich bread, crusts removed
2 whole eggs, plus 3 yolks
4 tablespoons sugar
500 ml (17 fl oz) milk
500 ml (17 fl oz) whipping cream
1 vanilla pod, split in two
100 g (3¹/₂ oz) sultanas

Preheat the oven to 160°C (325°F) gas mark 3.
Cut the bread in pieces and put in an ovenproof dish.
Whisk the eggs and sugar until the mixture turns pale and foamy. Meantime, put the milk and cream into a saucepan, add the vanilla pod and bring to the boil.
Remove the vanilla pod and pour the hot milk over the eggs, stirring well.
Scrape out the vanilla pod and add the seeds to the milk–egg mixture. Add the sultanas and pour over the bread, leave to swell for 20 minutes.
Cook for around 40 minutes. Serve warm or cold.

Pear and cranberry crumble

Serves 6
Preparation time: 15 minutes
Cooking time: 45 minutes

100 g (3¹/₂ oz) granulated sugar
225 g (7 oz) flour
175 g (6 oz) butter
5 ripe pears, peeled and diced
150 g (5 oz) cranberries
2–3 tablespoons molasses sugar

Preheat the oven to 190°C (375°F) gas mark 5.
In a large bowl, rub the sugar, flour and butter through your fingers until the mixture resembles breadcrumbs.
Put the pears and the cranberries in an ovenproof dish, sprinkle with the crumble mixture and the molasses sugar.
Bake in the oven for around 45 minutes.

Best of British

A party with a traditional flavour, that gets away from all those fusion, oriental or Italian menus.

My French guests love this version of British cooking that sweeps away long-held prejudices formed during their first language school experiences.

There's great scope for dressing-up, too: any style, from the old-but-good-kilt-I-couldn't-bear-to-throw-out to the 'We will always love you Diana' T-shirt, by way of the latest creations of Paul Smith, Burberry or Galliano.

For me, it's an apron from Cath Kidston or Harvey Nicks, *puh-leeze*.

Royal Pimms

Summer fruits: strawberries,
raspberries, cherries
sprigs of mint
$1/3$ Pimms
$2/3$ Champagne
ice cubes

Put the fruit in a tumbler. Pour the Pimms
over, then the Champagne and add ice
cubes and mint.

Beef and horseradish

Makes 12 small sandwiches
Preparation time: 5 minutes

3–4 teaspoons of horseradish sauce or 3 teaspoons
of crème fraîche or mascarpone mixed with 1 teaspoon
of puréed horseradish
100 g (3$\frac{1}{2}$ oz) cooked roast beef, sliced very thinly
6 slices of bread: white sandwich, brown or wholemeal

Spread the horseradish sauce on 3 slices of bread. Put a slice
of beef on each, and top with the remaining bread. Cut off
the crusts and cut the sandwiches into 4 triangles or fingers.

Double salmon

Makes 12 small sandwiches
Cooking time: 2 minutes
Preparation time: 5 minutes

150 g (5 oz) salmon fillet, steamed or microwaved
50 g (2 oz) smoked salmon
1 tablespoon crème fraîche or mascarpone
2 tablespoons lemon juice
1 teaspoon dill, chopped
1 teaspoon chives, chopped
6 slices bread – white, brown or wholemeal

Chop all the salmon and mix with the crème fraîche, lemon
juice and herbs.
Spread on 3 slices of bread, top with the other slices, remove
crusts and cut into 4 triangles or fingers.

Ham and Cheddar

Makes 12 small sandwiches
Preparation time: 5 minutes

50 g (2 oz) softened unsalted butter
6 slices bread (white, brown or wholemeal)
3 slices ham
150 g (5 oz) Cheddar cheese, finely sliced

Butter 3 slices of bread. Lay a slice of ham on each, then a
slice of cheese. Top with the remaining 3 slices of bread.
Remove the crusts and cut into 4 triangles or into fingers.

Corned beef with two tomatoes

Makes 12 small sandwiches
Preparation time: 10 minutes

1 tomato
1 semi-dried tomato in oil
1 small can corned beef, finely chopped
2 tablespoons Worcestershire sauce
6 slices of white bread
sea salt, pepper

Plunge the fresh tomato into boiling water for 30 seconds,
then into cold, and peel. Chop finely with the semi-dried
tomato and mix with the corned beef. The juice and oil
of the tomatoes will give the mixture a smooth texture.
Season with salt, pepper and Worcestershire sauce.
Spread on 3 slices of bread, cover with the remaining three
slices. Remove the crusts and cut into 4 triangles or fingers.

Dressed crab

Dressed crab with yogurt, coriander and lime, salad of rocket and baby spinach, melba toast

Ah, melba toast, that speciality of Northern Irish restaurants in the 1970s! It looked lovely but was impossible to butter. Nowadays it's retro enough to make a comeback.

Not so long ago, my Northern Irish compatriots disliked cooking or preparing fish and seafood. They always bought it filleted and pan-fried or 'dressed' it – hence the name of this dish. But tastes evolve and nowadays lobsters, langoustines and oysters are not exported from Ireland to France in such great quantities as formerly. For this recipe, if you are cooking for many, it will save time if you buy crabmeat already taken off the shell.

Serves 6 as a small starter or 12 as a canapé
Preparation time: 25 minutes
Resting time: 30 minutes

150 g (5 oz) crabmeat
2 tablespoons natural Greek yogurt
2 tablespoons fresh coriander, finely chopped
1 tablespoon fresh basil, finely chopped
juice of $\frac{1}{2}$ lime
$1\frac{1}{2}$ tablespoons desiccated coconut
3 slices of day-old white bread
a few handfuls of rocket and baby spinach
sea salt and pepper

Preheat the grill.
Mix together the crabmeat, yogurt, herbs, lime juice and coconut, and season.
Set aside for 30 minutes to let the herbs diffuse their aromas. Remove the crusts from the bread and toast both sides lightly under the grill. Using a sharp knife cut through each slice horizontally. This is a rather delicate operation but don't panic if they don't come out as 6 perfect, thin slices. You will be breaking them up afterwards. Just make sure that they're big enough to retrieve if they get stuck on the grill.
Put the untoasted sides back under the grill and toast lightly. Set aside to cool.
Put a few salad leaves in glasses or bowls, add half a tablespoon of the crabmeat mixture to each, top with a piece of melba toast, and serve.

Ploughman's lunch

How rare it is to find this great pub speciality served up as it should be: a big plate of carrot and celery sticks, decent cheese, homemade chutney, pickled onions and good bread. It's a very practical starter, just provide the complete kit so that everyone can make their own sandwiches or simply munch a few crudités.

Serves 10
Preparation time: 20 minutes

4 carrots, cut into batons
4 celery sticks, sliced into batons
10 small hearts of lettuce
20 radishes
20 small pickled onions
300 g (10 oz) Stilton cheese
300 g (10 oz) Cheddar cheese
butter
5 tablespoons chutney
good bread cut into rustic chunks

Arrange all the ingredients on a board or a pretty platter. Remember to provide knives and small plates so that everyone can help themselves.

Cheesy potato with Cheddar and sweetcorn

Makes 20 portions
Cooking time: 25 minutes
Preparation time: 20 minutes

10 small firm-fleshed potatoes
1 medium can sweetcorn
200 g (7 oz) grated Cheddar cheese
50 g (2 oz) butter, melted
salt and pepper

Boil the potatoes unpeeled.
When cooked, slice in half and take out a little of the potato to make a small well in the centre. Cut a sliver from the uncut side of each potato so that they will stand firm.
Mix the potato with the sweetcorn, cheese and butter. Season, and top each half-potato with a spoonful of the mixture, then brown for 3 minutes under the grill.

Cheesy potato with Cheddar and sweetcom

Bloody Mary soup

Serves 8
Cooking time: 50 minutes
Preparation time: 10 minutes

1 kg (2 lb) ripe tomatoes, peeled
2 celery sticks, sliced
1 tablespoon sugar
olive oil
2 teaspoons concentrated tomato purée
vodka
Tabasco
Worcestershire sauce
sea salt and black pepper

Put the tomatoes in a bowl with the celery and sugar and season lightly. Cover and leave to marinate for around 40 minutes then add the tomato purée and the olive oil. Blend in a liquidizer, adding a little water if the soup is too thick. Chill well before adding vodka to taste.
Serve chilled, with celery sticks. Your guests can season to taste with Tabasco, Worcestershire sauce, salt and pepper.

Partan bree

This is a traditional Scottish soup that requires some work in removing the crabmeat from its shell. It's not too difficult, however.

Serves 8
Cooking time: 30 minutes
Preparation time: 25 minutes

1 cooked crab, weighing about 1.5–1.8kg (3–3$\frac{1}{2}$ lb)
1 celery stick, diced
1 carrot, cut into rounds
1 turnip, halved
2 shallots, finely chopped
50 g (2 oz) long-grain rice
500 ml (17 fl oz) milk
500 ml (17 fl oz) whipping cream
1 tablespoon Worcestershire sauce
2 or 3 teaspoons Scotch whisky (optional)

Extract the crabmeat from the shell and set aside. Put the carcass in a saucepan with the vegetables, cover with water and simmer for around 25 minutes.
Pass the crab stock through a fine sieve then reduce by boiling if necessary to obtain 500–750 ml (17 fl oz–1$\frac{1}{4}$ pints) of stock. Reserve several pieces of the claws for decoration. Simmer the rice and milk in another saucepan for around 20 minutes until all the milk is absorbed. Put in a food processor along with the crabmeat and stock and process well. Before serving, add the cream and season to taste. Add the Worcestershire sauce and whisky and reheat gently.
Decorate with meat from the crab claws and serve with Scottish oatcakes.

Cream of petits pois with almonds, toast and preserved lemon

Serves 6
Preparation time: 30 minutes
Cooking time: 10 minutes

For the soup:
2 kg (4 lb) fresh unshelled petits pois or 500 g (1 lb) frozen
1 litre (1$\frac{3}{4}$ pints) chicken or vegetable stock
50 g (2 oz) whole almonds, blanched and peeled
150 ml ($\frac{1}{4}$ pint) whipping cream

For the toast:
150 g (5 oz) softened unsalted butter
50 g (2 oz) preserved lemon, finely chopped
15 small slices country bread, toasted
1 or 2 sprigs of chervil, to decorate

Shell the peas and cook in the stock for 10 minutes; if frozen, cook as indicated on the packet.
Add the almonds and blend the soup well in a liquidizer. Stir in the cream, adding water if necessary to adjust the consistency. Mix the butter with the lemon. Serve in a pretty butter-dish with the toast and let everyone help themself.
The soup can be made ahead of time and reheated before serving. Decorate with a few sprigs of chervil.

Tip • Chicken stock gives the best flavour, but if you are pressed for time, make an 'express' stock with 2 litres (3$\frac{1}{2}$ pints) of water, 1 carrot, 1 stick celery, 1 onion and a bay leaf. Peel and dice the vegetables and boil over a lively heat for at least 30 minutes, then press through a fine sieve. This goes much better with the delicate petits pois than stock cubes or powder.

Parsnip and apple soup with saffron and cumin

Parsnip's sweetish taste, halfway between carrot and celeriac, goes well with spices.

Serves 6
Preparation time: 15 minutes
Cooking time: 50 minutes

1 pinch saffron
2 tablespoons olive oil
100 g (3$\frac{1}{2}$ oz) onions, diced
800 g (1$\frac{1}{2}$ lb) parsnips, peeled and diced
1 litre (1$\frac{3}{4}$ pints) water
250 g (8 oz) apples, peeled and diced
2 teaspoons cumin
salt and pepper

Soak the saffron in 2 tablespoons of hot water.
Heat the olive oil in a saucepan and sweat the onions.
Add the parsnip and cook a few minutes longer, then add the water. Cook for 30 minutes more then add the apples and cook for a further 10 minutes. Take off the heat, blend in a liquidizer, add the saffron water and cumin. Add more water if the mixture is too thick. Season to taste and serve.

Coronation chicken

Beef and beer ragout with Cheddar croûtons

Breakfast omelette

Coronation chicken

This is my version of a dish created to mark the Coronation of Queen Elizabeth II. It's delicious and very practical.

Serves 6
Preparation time: 10 minutes
Cooking time: 20 minutes
Chilling time: 30 minutes

500 ml (17 fl oz) water
500 ml (17 fl oz) white wine
2 bay leaves
1 stick celery
1 carrot, diced
1 small onion
6 boneless, skinless chicken breasts
salt and pepper

For the sauce:
2 tablespoons mayonnaise
250 ml (8 fl oz) whipping cream
1 tablespoon sun-dried tomato purée
1–2 tablespoons curry sauce (preferably korma or tikka)

Bring to the boil the water, wine and all other ingredients except the chicken. Reduce the heat and add the chicken breasts and poach for about 20 minutes. Remove from the bouillon and leave to cool, then cut into bite-sized pieces. Mix the sauce ingredients together thoroughly and add the chicken, stirring to coat each piece. Serve chilled, accompanied with basmati rice, flavoured with cardamom seeds and the grated rind of 1 lemon, if desired.

Tip • For the photograph I decorated the dish with Pan Masala, available from Indian grocery stores.

Beef and beer ragout with Cheddar croûtons

Serves 6
Preparation time: 20 minutes
Cooking time: 2^1/$_2$ to 3 hours

4 onions, finely chopped
3 tablespoons olive oil
1 kg (2 lb) lean stewing steak, cubed
1 tablespoon flour
500 ml (17 fl oz) beer
500 ml (17 fl oz) water
3 celery sticks, sliced
2 carrots, sliced into rounds
2 tablespoons tomato purée
2 bay leaves
1 baguette
150 g (5 oz) Cheddar or Stilton cheese, grated
pinch of salt

To season:
sea salt, freshly milled black pepper
HP or Worcestershire sauce

Preheat the oven to 150°C (300°F) gas mark 2.
In a flameproof casserole that you can bring to the table, gently soften and colour the onions in the oil then add the meat. When it is browned all over, add the flour and cook gently for a further 1–2 minutes. Add more oil if necessary. Add all the other ingredients and mix well, scraping up any sticking to the bottom. Bring to the boil then transfer to the oven and cook for around 2^1/$_2$ hours. Adjust the seasoning with HP or Worcestershire sauce, salt and pepper.
To make the croûtons: 20 minutes before serving, slice the baguette into rounds, sprinkle with cheese and put the croûtons on top of the ragout. Turn up the temperature to 180°C (350°F) gas mark 4 for 20 minutes then serve.

Tip • The ragout can be prepared the night before or left to go cold. It will only improve. Reheat it before adding the croûtons if you don't want to serve it cold.

Breakfast omelette

Serves 6
Preparation time: 5 minutes
Cooking time: 15 minutes

2 pork sausages cut into rounds
150 g (5 oz) bacon, diced
4–5 button mushrooms, sliced
2 tomatoes, deseeded
8 eggs, lightly whisked
salt and pepper

Heat a non-stick frying pan and fry the sausages, then the bacon, the mushrooms and finally the tomatoes, cooking each for a few minutes in turn. Then add the eggs, a little salt and pepper and cook gently for 5–7 minutes.
Slide the omelette onto a plate and serve hot, warm or cold.

Stilton terrine with two pears

Serves 6–8
Preparation time: 20 minutes
Chilling time: 3–4 hours

150 g (5 oz) dried pears, sliced
300–350 g (10–12 oz) Stilton cheese, crust removed
and crumbled
4–5 slices wholemeal bread, crust removed
3 ripe pears (eg Comice), peeled and diced

Line a small terrine with clingfilm and place the slices of
dried pears neatly along the base, as this will be on top when
presented for serving. (Do not use a flexible mould as you
want the mixture to be shaped by the sides.)
Divide the Stilton into 2 equal portions and place 1 portion
in a layer over the dried pears.
Cut the bread to fit, divide into 3 equal portions and press
1 portion down firmly over the cheese.
Put the fresh pears on top of this layer of bread, cover with
a second layer of bread and add the second layer of cheese.
Finish with a layer of the remaining bread.
Cover with a piece of foil or greaseproof paper, then a piece
of stiff card cut to fit. Place a heavy weight (full jars or cans,
if you don't have a weight) onto the card.
Refrigerate for at least 3 or 4 hours, overnight if you can.
Turn out carefully from the terrine onto a pretty plate and
serve with a crisp green salad and walnuts or hazelnuts.

Upsidedown summer pudding

Christmas pudding ice cream

Upsidedown summer pudding

This is a great British classic, not at all like those stodgy boiled puddings that have such a bad reputation. Here I've suggested making it in individual portions to save turning out.

Serves 6–8
Preparation time: 25 minutes
Cooking time: 15 minutes
Chilling time: overnight

700–800 g (1^1/$_2$–1^3/$_4$ lb) summer fruits (strawberries, raspberries, blackberries, blackcurrants, cherries, gooseberries).
75–100 g (3–3^1/$_2$ oz) sugar, depending on ripeness of the fruit
8–10 slices day-old white sandwich bread, crusts removed
whipping cream
mascarpone cheese (optional)

Reserving some of the best for decoration, put all the fruit except the strawberries and raspberries in a saucepan with the sugar and 100 ml (3^1/$_2$ fl oz) water. Cook gently, stirring until the sugar dissolves.
Add the remaining fruits, halving the strawberries if large, and cook for a further 5 minutes. The fruit should be poached without losing its shape. Leave to cool for around 15 minutes.
Cut the bread slices into triangles and line the bottom and sides of small individual ramekins or tumblers. Carefully spoon in the poached fruit. Chill overnight in the refrigerator.
Decorate with the reserved fruit and serve with whipped cream into which, if you wish, you have stirred a tablespoonful of mascarpone and a little sugar.

Christmas pudding ice cream

The pudding flavour mingles with the ice cream for a party dessert that is much easier to make than a real pudding (and without the suet!)

Serves 8–10
Preparation time: 15 minutes
Steeping time: overnight
Chilling time: 1 hour

2 tablespoons candied mixed fruits, diced
2 tablespoons candied orange peel, diced
2 tablespoons currants
2 tablespoons raisins
1 tablespoon walnuts, finely chopped
5 tablespoons rum
3 tablespoons port
grated rind of 1 orange
grated rind of ^{1}/$_2$ lemon and 2 tablespoons juice
1 teaspoon ground mixed spice
1 litre (1^3/$_4$ pints) good-quality vanilla ice cream

Mix together all the ingredients, except the ice cream, in a bowl, cover and leave steeping overnight in the refrigerator. Take the ice cream from the freezer and let it soften slightly before stirring into the fruit mixture.
Return the bowl to the freezer for an hour or so until the ice cream firms up again.

Real sherry trifle

Serves 8–10
Preparation time: 15 minutes
Cooking time: 30 minutes
Chilling time: 3 hours

4 tablespoons cherry jam
20 sponge finger biscuits
5 tablespoons sherry
2 bananas, peeled and sliced into rounds
grated rind of ^{1}/$_2$ lemon and 2 tablespoons of juice
200 g (7 oz) pitted black preserved cherries
5 egg yolks
50 g (2 oz) sugar
500 ml (17 fl oz) milk
200 ml (7 fl oz) whipping cream
3 tablespoons mascarpone
3 tablespoons flaked almonds, toasted

Spread cherry jam on the sponge fingers and arrange in a dish. Pour over the sherry. Soak the sliced bananas in the lemon juice to keep them from turning brown and layer them on top of the biscuits. Arrange the cherries on top.
Beat the egg yolks and sugar together until the mixture turns pale. Bring the milk to the boil, take off the heat and pour over the egg yolk mixture stirring constantly. Return the custard to the pan and cook gently *without* boiling until it thickens, stirring constantly. Set aside until completely cold then pour over the fruit.
Whip the cream lightly, stir in the mascarpone and pour over the custard. Decorate with the toasted almonds.

After Eight mousse – and matching mint

When marketing men, in a frenzy of niche retailing, created After Eight mints, I couldn't resist paying homage to all those restaurant menus with their rather pompous dishes.

Serves 8–10
Preparation time: 10 minutes
Chilling time: 2 hours

For the mousse:
500 ml (17 fl oz) whipping cream
15 After Eight mints

To decorate:
10 After Eight mints

Bring the cream to boiling point, remove from the heat and beat in the 15 After Eight mint chocolates, using a wire whisk, until they are all melted. Chill in the refrigerator for 2 hours. Whip the mousse with an electric beater until it peaks. Pour into little cups or ramekins and decorate each with a matching mint chocolate!

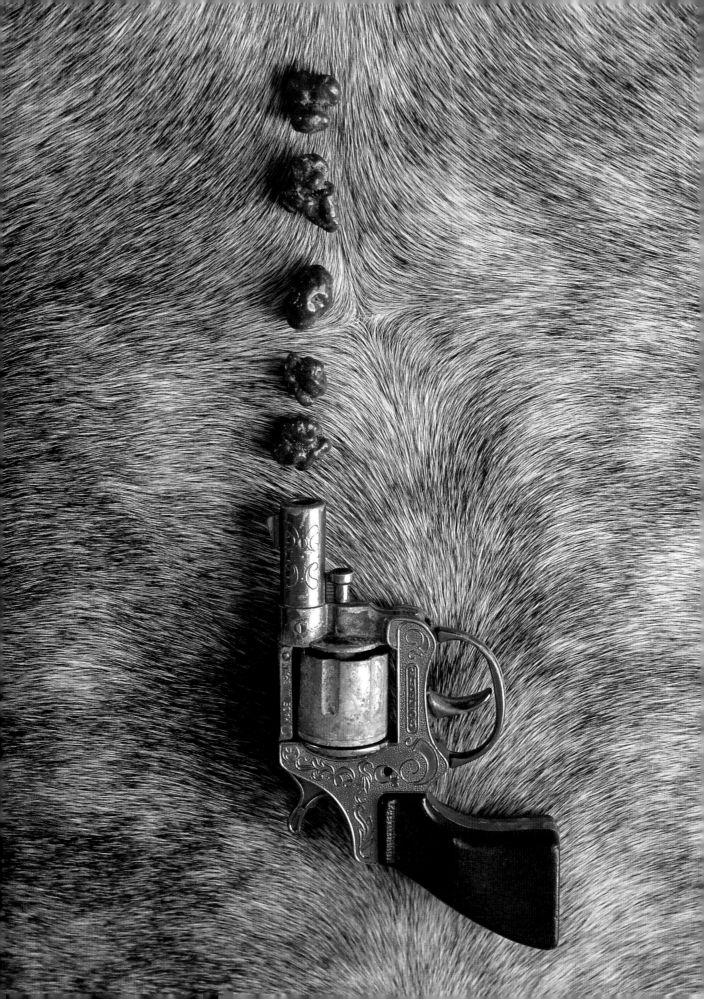

Western

One of my most unforgettable parties was a Western barbecue thrown in bleak January by Diane, alias Dolly, and Alain, alias Big Al, the celebrated organizers of the first and last genuine Halloween party, three years before the rest of the country sank under a commercial orgy of yellow and black plastic.

Sixty-eight people crammed into as many square metres, an enormous margarita was handed to each guest almost before the horses were hitched, a gigantic and efficient barbecue was installed in an outside temperature of 5°C (-15°F) under a small marquee attached to the French windows of the room set aside for dancing.

Plus, the dressing up involved minimum stress, expense or feeling foolish. Everyone's got a pair of jeans or a checked shirt. Even a Zorro outfit would do the trick.

The food is also easy to prepare: good tacos, homemade burgers and a few corny ice creams. All the same, I have thrown in a few other good ideas.

Steak sandwich with BBQ sauce

Serves 8
Preparation time: 20 minutes
Cooking time: 5 minutes

2 x 100 g (3$\frac{1}{2}$ oz) steaks, beaten flat
5 teaspoons sea salt
2 teaspoons black pepper
3 teaspoons ground cumin
12 thick slices country bread
olive oil
1 bottle BBQ sauce

Coat the steaks with a mixture of the salt, pepper and cumin
and set aside.
Cut the bread in two and make a hollow in the centre for the
meat. Just before serving, heat the olive oil in a cast-iron pan
and fry the steaks rapidly, then cut them into bite-size morsels.
Lay them on the bread, anoint liberally with the sauce and
close with another slice of bread.
Cut into fingers and serve hot.

Nachos

Serves 8
Preparation time: 10 minutes
Cooking time: 10 minutes

2 large ripe avocados, peeled and roughly chopped
1 large tomato, peeled, deseeded and finely diced
4 tablespoons lemon juice
1 garlic clove, crushed
1 large packet of tortilla chips
1 large jar salsa sauce, mild or piquant
200 g (7 oz) Cheddar cheese, grated
3–4 tablespoons crème fraîche
salt and pepper

Prepare the guacamole by mixing together the avocado,
tomato, lemon juice and garlic. Blend in a liquidizer to
a smooth purée and season to taste
Preheat the oven to 180°C (350°F) gas mark 4.
Put the chips in a large ovenproof dish. Pour the salsa over,
sprinkle with grated Cheddar then put in the oven until the
cheese melts over the chips. Serve accompanied by the
guacamole and crème fraîche.

Lobster roll

On this side of the Atlantic, it may seem rather shocking to
use lobster in a hot dog with mayonnaise. Never mind, it's
delicious.

Serves 4
Preparation time: 25 minutes, or however long it takes
to extract the lobster meat
Reheating time: 2 minutes for the bread

450 g (14 oz) lobster meat
1 x 10-cm (4-inch) celery stick, finely diced
4 tablespoons readymade mayonnaise
grated rind of 1 lemon
4 tablespoons lemon juice
4 hot dog rolls
salt and pepper

Mix the lobster meat with all the other ingredients except
the rolls. The rolls should be gently warmed, in the oven
or the microwave – whatever's handiest.
Fill the rolls and serve.

Peanut butter and jelly sandwich

Everyone dismisses this combination, yet the crunchy sweet-
salty-savoury mixture is terrific. Just don't butter the bread
before spreading the peanut butter. Enough's enough!
Americans mainly use grape jelly, but any flavour of jam or jelly
is fine – it's up to you.

Makes 24 sandwiches
Preparation time: 5 minutes

12 slices of sandwich bread, white or wholemeal
1 jar crunchy peanut butter
1 jar redcurrant jelly

Spread the peanut butter on 6 slices of bread, then add a layer
of jelly. Cover with the remaining 6 slices and cut into four.

Rice salad with black beans and hot salsa

Swordfish ceviche

Prawn, mango and peanut salad

Rice salad with black beans and hot salsa

Here's a rice salad with a twist …

Serves 10
Cooking time: 10 minutes, for the rice
Preparation time: 20 minutes

1 kg (2 lb) white rice, cooked
2 x 400-g (14-oz) cans black beans, or black-eyed beans
1 x 340-g (11-oz) can sweetcorn
150 ml (5 fl oz) olive oil
1 tablespoon cumin powder
5 tomatoes, peeled
2 red peppers
5 shallots
2 garlic cloves
2 red chillies
3 tablespoons lime juice
1 bunch fresh coriander, chopped
1 bunch basil, chopped
salt and pepper

Cook the rice and set aside to cool. Drain and rinse the black beans. Drain the sweetcorn. Mix both into the rice, adding 4 tablespoons of the olive oil and cumin. Season to taste and set aside for the flavours to mingle.
Deseed the peeled tomatoes and dice the flesh finely.
Dice the peppers, shallots, garlic and the chillies.
Mix all the vegetables with the lime juice and remaining olive oil and season.
Arrange on the rice and garnish with coriander and basil.

Note • If you wish to peel the peppers and chillies, roast in a hot oven until the skins blacken and blister. Put in a polythene bag, seal and leave for about 10 minutes to sweat the skins, which should then peel easily. If you don't want the salsa too hot, deseed the chillies.

Swordfish *ceviche*

Serves 8 (as a starter)
Preparation time: 45 minutes

400 g (13 oz) swordfish or tuna – tell your fishmonger you want to serve it raw, to make sure it's very fresh
juice of 3 limes
200 g (7 oz) red onions, sliced into fine strips
2 red peppers, roasted, peeled, deseeded and finely diced
2 tablespoons flat leaf parsley, finely chopped
1 tablespoon coriander, finely chopped
2 garlic cloves, very finely diced
$1/2$ red chilli, very finely diced (optional)
2 limes, sliced into very thin rounds, to decorate

Slice the raw fish into thin strips and marinate in the lime juice for 30 minutes.
Mix together all the other ingredients, then finally add the marinated fish.
Serve well-chilled, garnished with slices of lime.

Prawn, mango and peanut salad

Serves 6
Preparation time: 10 minutes

For the sauce:
4 tablespoons mayonnaise
2 tablespoons mango chutney
1 teaspoon cumin powder
1 teaspoon ground ginger
juice of 1 lime
sea salt, freshly milled black pepper

1 kg (2 lb) cooked, peeled prawns
1 ripe mango, peeled and diced
1 packet lettuce hearts, or 2 Little Gem lettuces
3 tablespoons dry-roasted peanuts
1 bunch fresh coriander

Mix together all the sauce ingredients then add the prawns and mango. Line a bowl with the lettuce leaves and add the prawn mixture.
Sprinkle with peanuts and fresh coriander leaves.

New England chowder

Serves 6
Preparation time: 20 minutes
Cooking time: 15 minutes

3 shallots
50 g (2 oz) butter
30 g (1^1/$_4$ oz) flour
150 ml (^{1}/$_4$ pint) white wine
1 litre (1^3/$_4$ pints) good fish stock
1 kg (2 lb) mussels, cleaned
1 dozen clams, cleaned and in their shells
250 g (8 oz) cod or halibut, cut in pieces
5 tablespoons crème fraîche
salt and pepper

Sweat the shallots in the butter, add the flour and cook for
2 minutes.
Add the wine and fish stock. Boil for 2–3 minutes.
At this point you can set aside the bouillon and finish cooking
the chowder just before you are ready to serve.
Add the shellfish and the fish and cook for a further
10 minutes. Discard any mussels or clams that have not
opened.
Just before serving, add the crème fraîche. Serve with little
crackers.
To make a more substantial dish, you can add steamed
potatoes cut into small chunks.

Extra hot chilli

Serves 8
Preparation time: 15 minutes
Cooking time: 1^1/$_2$–2 hours

2 tablespoons olive oil
2 onions, chopped
4 garlic cloves, diced
2 carrots, sliced
1 tablespoon ground cumin
1 tablespoon dried oregano
1.5 kg (3 lb) minced lean beef
1 x 400-g (14-oz) can chopped tomatoes
1 small can concentrated tomato paste
1 tablespoon sugar
2 tablespoons good chilli powder
^{1}/$_2$ teaspoon Cayenne pepper
1 litre (1^3/$_4$ pints) beef bouillon or stock
1 teaspoon salt
1 large can kidney beans, rinsed and drained
parsley
crème fraîche

Heat the oil in a large saucepan. Add the onions, garlic,
carrots, cumin and oregano. Cook over a low heat for
5 minutes.
Turn up the heat, add the meat and turn it in the oil until
it is sealed and browned all over.
Add canned tomatoes, tomato paste, sugar, chilli powder,
Cayenne pepper, the bouillon or stock and salt. Simmer
uncovered for around 1 hour.
When the chilli has thickened, add the kidney beans and
parsley. Cover and cook for a further 10 minutes.
Just before serving, add one or two tablespoons of
crème fraîche.
Serve with hot tortillas and bowls of crème fraîche,
salad and grated Cheddar cheese.

Pecan and maple syrup tart

Serves 8
Preparation time: 10 minutes, pastry; 10 minutes, filling
Chilling time: 2 hours, for the pastry
Cooking time: 35–40 minutes

Short crust pastry:
(to make a pastry case around 28 cm (11 inches) in diameter)
250 g (8 oz) flour
125 g (4 oz) butter, chilled
2 tablespoons sugar
3–4 tablespoons iced water

Put the flour, butter and sugar in a mixer and process until the mixture resembles breadcrumbs. Add the water gradually, as you may not need all of it, and process for a few seconds more. Do not over-process.
Draw the dough into a ball, put in a polythene bag, and leave to rest for 2 hours in the refrigerator.
When ready to cook, take the pastry out of the refrigerator to soften. Preheat the oven to 190°C (375 °F) gas mark 5. Roll out the dough and line a greased baking tin. Return to the refrigerator while preparing the filling.

The filling:
60 g (2^1/$_2$ oz) melted butter
100 g (3^1/$_2$ oz) sugar
175 ml (6 fl oz) maple syrup
2 eggs
250 g (8 oz) pecan nuts

Beat together the butter, sugar and maple syrup. Add the eggs, beating continually.
Layer the pecans in the uncooked pastry case and pour over the filling. Spread the nuts evenly over the pastry.
Bake for 15 minutes at 190°C (375 °F) gas mark 5 then lower the temperature to 170°C (338 °F) gas mark 3–4 and bake for a further 25–30 minutes.
Cool, and serve warm or cold.

Maple syrup pancakes

Most supermarkets stock these pancakes nowadays. I know that the ones in the photograph *opposite* are British-made but they're very like genuine American pancakes. Just reheat them gently in the oven or under the grill and serve with maple syrup and a good vanilla ice cream.

Blondies

Makes 30 squares
Preparation time: 15 minutes
Cooking time: 25 minutes

175 g (6 oz) butter, softened
300 g (10 oz) soft brown sugar
150 g (5 oz) caster or granulated sugar
3 eggs + 1 yolk
100 g (3^1/$_2$ oz) crunchy peanut butter
400 g (13 oz) flour
1 teaspoon baking powder
325 g (11 oz) chocolate chips

Preheat the oven to 180°C (350°F) gas mark 4. Butter a square or rectangular baking tin. Beat together the butter and the two sugars until the mixture turns pale and creamy. Add the eggs and the single yolk one by one, beating all the time. Blend in the peanut butter, sift in the flour and baking powder. Add the chocolate chips, mix well, and pour the mixture into the tin.
Bake for 20–25 minutes. Take care not to overcook: the Blondies should be deliciously sticky.

Blueberry cobbler with American crumble

Serves 6–8
Preparation time: 10 minutes
Cooking time: 20 minutes

500 g (1 lb) blueberries
3 tablespoons sugar

For the cobbler:
3 tablespoons sugar
120 g (4 oz) flour
1^1/$_2$ teaspoons baking powder
1 egg, beaten
75 ml (3 fl oz) milk

Preheat the oven to 190°C (375°F) gas mark 5.
Put the fruit in an ovenproof dish and sprinkle with sugar. Mix together the sugar, flour and baking powder. Add the egg and the milk and mix well to obtain a smooth texture. Spoon over the fruit and bake for around 20 minutes.

Colours

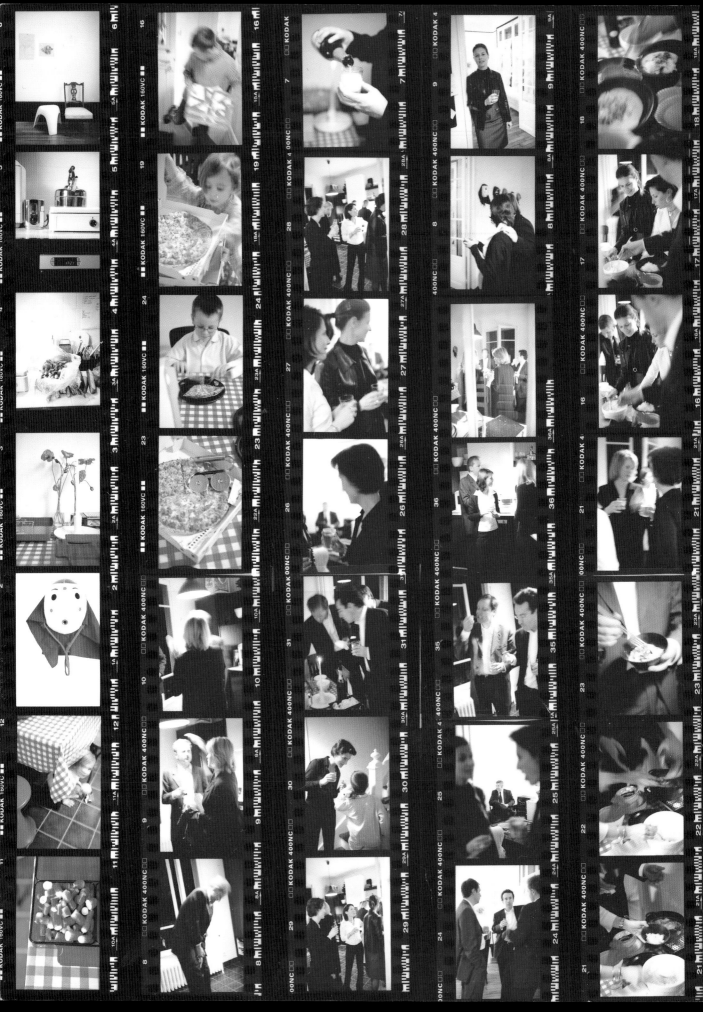

It's fun to focus on a colour when food-shopping. A whole meal – starter, main dish, dessert – can be created from all or any of the colours of the rainbow.

A party, however, hinges on variety and dishes that are easy to serve, but the constraints of colour can be an inspiration: they can lead the way to trying new things and to ultra-simplicity.

Nature plays its part, too. Every season has its own colour. Black and white for the festive season (caviar, truffles, foie gras, oysters), green for springtime (fresh herbs, petits pois and spring vegetables), pink for the beginning of summer (langoustine, rhubarb, strawberries, salmon) and orange for autumn (pumpkins, oranges).

Your guests' colour coordination can be minimal. Anyone can dig out a scarf, handkerchief or tie in the featured colour. As for the décor, single-colour flowers, fruits and vegetables on a colour-coordinated buffet and white or clear glass crockery will harmonize elegantly with your menus.

black & white

Shots

A small selection of 'shots',
powerful mini-cocktails to down
in one as if you were still 18.

Black dragon
$\frac{1}{3}$ whisky
$\frac{1}{3}$ kahlua
$\frac{1}{3}$ crème de menthe

Black samurai
1 measure sake
1 dash soy sauce

Black tooth
$\frac{2}{3}$ whisky
$\frac{1}{3}$ Coca-Cola

Black orchid
$\frac{1}{3}$ grenadine
$\frac{1}{3}$ white rum
$\frac{1}{3}$ curaçao

Cheeses and dried fruits
Corsican or Basque Tome cheese with black cherry jam
Quail eggs with poppy seeds
Oysters with caviar

Appetizers

Corsican or Basque Tome cheese with black cherry jam

Serve this in 'kit' form. Provide small chunks of bread and serve the jam in a little bowl with a spoon and the cheese with a knife, so that everyone can dig in as they please. If you can't get Tome, use goats' cheese or Lancashire.

Quail eggs with poppy seeds

quail eggs
poppy seeds
sea salt

Hard-boil the eggs. Peel off the tops. Serve accompanied by a bowl of poppy seeds mixed with sea salt and another receptacle for the eggshells.

Oysters with caviar

For 24 oysters

50 g (2 oz) caviar – more if your budget permits.

Open the oysters. Arrange them on a bed of black or white pebbles, or even coarse salt. Top each oyster with a few grains of caviar.

Foie gras morsels

Fill a small spoon with aspic topped with a mouthful of raw or part-cooked foie gras. Sprinkle with sea salt and pepper.

Salt cod purée (*brandade*) and pepper sandwiches

Makes 12 small sandwiches

1 pot of *brandade*, or smoked mackerel pâté
6 slices white sandwich bread
pepper

Spread the *brandade* on the bread, remove the crusts and cut into long slices.
Sprinkle with pepper – perhaps a bit less than in the photograph! Brandade is a purée made from salt cod.

Tapenade sandwiches

Makes 20 sandwiches

10 slices white sandwich bread
1 small pot tapenade (black olive purée)

Spread the tapenade in a light layer on half the bread. Top with the rest of the bread, cut off the crusts and slice the sandwiches lengthways into fingers.

Rice cakes with black radish

Makes 10 cakes

1 black radish (more, depending on size)
150 g (5 oz) butter
10 rice cakes

Slice the radish in very thin rounds.
Butter the rice cakes and arrange the radish slices artistically on them.

Roasted, rolled aubergines with tomato and cream cheese

2–3 large aubergines
1 jar tomato conserve
1 carton Saint-Moret, or Philadelphia cream cheese

Roast the aubergines in a hot oven until cooked through but not mushy. Allow to cool completely and then cut into thin slices.
Spread a little tomato conserve over. Not too much, so that the red doesn't show.
Spread with cheese, roll up and close with a toothpick.

Rollmops

Makes 12 rollmops

1 jar plain rollmops
12 toothpicks

Cut the rollmop fillets into slices then roll them around the little pickled onions that they come with, or buy loose rollmops from a deli counter and a jar of silverskin onions.

Foie gras morsels

Rice cakes with black radish

Salt cod purée (*brandade*) and pepper sandwiches
+ Tapenade sandwiches

Roasted, rolled aubergines with
tomato and cream cheese

Cream of cauliflower with horn of plenty mushrooms

Potato soup with truffle butter

Cream of cauliflower with horn of plenty mushrooms

Serves 8
Preparation time: 15 minutes
Cooking time: 25 minutes

1 large cauliflower divided into florets or 1 large packet
frozen cauliflower florets
milk or water
150 g (5 oz) fresh wild mushrooms (horn of plenty or
chanterelles) or around 50 g (2 oz) dried, rehydrated
3 shallots, finely chopped
50 g (2 oz) butter
whipping cream
salt and pepper

Boil or steam the cauliflower florets until well done.
Blend the florets, adding enough milk or water to obtain
a soupy consistency. Season to taste.
Just before serving, brown the mushrooms and shallots lightly
in the butter. Stir a little cream into each bowl of hot soup
and top with a spoonful of the mushrooms and shallots.

Cream of asparagus with lemon

Serves 8
Preparation time: 15 minutes
Cooking time: 20 minutes

3 bundles fresh white asparagus or 2 packets frozen
white asparagus
1 litre (1³/₄ pints) chicken bouillon or stock
1 litre (1³/₄ pints) water
200 ml (7 fl oz) whipping cream
grated rind of 2 lemons
sea salt and pepper

Peel the asparagus, if using fresh.
Cook in the bouillon and water.
When cooked, blend in batches in a liquidizer, using
sufficient of the cooking liquid to make a soup consistency.
Add the cream, stir in the lemon rind and season to taste.

Potato soup with truffle butter

I detest culinary snobbery but I strongly advise you to buy only
good, fresh truffles.

A perfectly fresh, good quality truffle is more economical as it
is extremely powerful. The aroma is so strong that one or
two grated slivers will deliver a fabulous taste. To go with it,
I prefer simple accompaniments: hard-boiled or scrambled
eggs, creamed potatoes or potato soup, raw scallops or bread,
butter and sea salt.

Beware the truffles long-frozen, steeped in port, sold in some
delicatessens. Avoid the Christmas period when prices soar.
Only truffles gathered less than 10 days earlier and carefully
conserved will keep their aroma intact. If you live a long way
from a truffle region, ask your gourmet delicatessen to order
or choose a fine one just for you from their supplier.

Makes 12 small bowls
Preparation time: 30 minutes
Cooking time: 30 minutes

2 onions finely chopped
knob of butter
750 g (1¹/₂ lb) potatoes
500 ml (17 fl oz) chicken or vegetable bouillon, or stock
500 ml (17 fl oz) milk
¹/₂ fresh black truffle, weighing 25–30 g (1–1¹/₂ oz)
200 g (7 oz) good salted butter, softened
100 ml (3¹/₂ fl oz) whipping cream
sea salt

Cook the chopped onions gently in the butter without letting
them colour.
Add the potatoes and cook for several minutes, then add the
bouillon or stock and the milk. Cook for a further 30 minutes,
until the potatoes are well done. Blend the mixture in a
liquidizer, season to taste, and set aside.
Grate the truffle over the 200 g (7 oz) of softened butter
in dish and blend well. Cover with clingfilm and set aside.
Just before serving, gently reheat the soup and add the cream,
then 50 g (2 oz) truffle butter, blending in well.
Pour the soup into dishes, glasses or bowls and serve, each
garnished with a knob of truffle butter. Leave the diners to
add their own salt depending upon how they like to taste
their truffle.

Steamed scallops, mashed potatoes and black pudding

Steamed scallops, mashed potatoes and black pudding

Serves 3-6 (depending on how hungry the guests are)
Preparation time: 15 minutes
Cooking time: 30 minutes

6 waxy potatoes
knob of butter
100 ml (3$^1/_2$ fl oz) whipping cream
1 small black pudding
6 scallops

Peel the potatoes and cook in boiling water for 25 minutes or until well done. Mash the potatoes with butter and cream.
Skin the black pudding and crumble it over the surface of a heated frying pan.
Cook briskly until it is cooked through and crunchy – but not burnt! Set aside.
Steam the scallops for 3–4 minutes. While they are steaming, reheat the mashed potato and spoon into small bowls or plates.
Put the scallops on top of the potatoes, scatter over the black pudding and serve.

Easy chicken and pasta

This is easier to eat with a fork than those pretty pastas with cuttlefish-ink that always seem to come in the shape of spaghetti, at least where I shop.

Serves 8
Cooking time: 25 minutes
Preparation time: 20 minutes

1 packet wild-mushroom-flavoured pasta
4 boneless, skinless chicken breasts
2 shallots, finely diced
1 tablespoon olive oil
400 g (13 oz) assorted mushrooms, fresh, frozen, or dried and rehydrated (button mushrooms, field, chanterelles, oyster, chestnut, trompettes, cèpes…)
200 ml (7 fl oz) whipping cream
salt and pepper

Cook the pasta according to instructions on packet and set to one side.
Poach the chicken breasts for about 5 minutes in lightly salted water then cut them into bite-sized pieces. Gently cook the shallots in the oil then add the mushrooms and cook for 10 minutes.
Add the chicken and the cream and warm through if serving immediately. Pour over the pasta and serve.
Everything can be prepared ahead of time and microwaved to reheat just before serving.

Brousse with olive oil

Serves 8
Preparation time: 2 minutes

1 pot of brousse, or ricotta
150 ml ($^1/_4$ pint) good olive oil
sea salt and freshly milled black pepper

Unmould the cheese and serve with the oil, salt, pepper and a good crusty bread.

Brousse with olive oil

Oreos with coconut ice cream and chocolate sauce

Serves 6
Preparation time: 10 minutes

For the chocolate sauce:
150 g (5 oz) good plain chocolate (70% chocolate solids)
300 ml (7 fl oz) whipping cream
100 ml (3$^1/_2$ fl oz) milk

12 plain Oreos biscuits (not chocolate-covered – not black enough, my son!)
1 tub good coconut ice cream

Break the chocolate into pieces and put in a heatproof bowl. Bring the cream and milk just to the boil and pour over the chocolate, stirring well. Put aside to chill in the refrigerator. For the photograph (page 89), I split the Oreos and filled them with ice cream, but if you are making large quantities, there's no need to spend ages in the kitchen doing fancy sculptures. Just top an Oreo with a scoop of ice cream and pour the sauce over, then serve.

Meringue with blackberries and blueberries

Makes 10 meringues
Preparation time: 10 minutes

300 ml ($^1/_2$ pint) whipping cream
3 tablespoons mascarpone cheese
sugar
meringues (see page 112)
300 g (10 oz) fresh blackberries
200 g (7 oz) fresh blueberries

Whip the cream with the mascarpone and a little sugar. Serve the meringues with the cream and fruit on the side, in 'kit' form, and let everyone help themselves.

Meringue with blackberries and blueberries

Floating islands

Lychee and pitahaya salad

Floating islands

Serves 6
Preparation time: 20 minutes
Cooking time: 15 minutes

For the custard:
500 ml (17 fl oz) milk
5 egg yolks
50 g (2 oz) sugar

For the floating islands:
6 egg whites
45 g (1³/₄ oz) sugar

Put the milk in a saucepan and bring it almost to boiling point. Beat the egg yolks and sugar, using an electric beater, until the mixture turns pale and doubles in volume. Pour the almost-boiling milk over, beating constantly. Return the custard to the saucepan over medium heat, stirring constantly with a wooden spoon until it coats the back of the spoon. Leave to cool then refrigerate.
Whisk the egg whites into peaks. Gradually add the sugar, whipping all the time.
Bring a large saucepan of water to a simmer and poach spoonfuls of whipped egg white by plunging them into the simmering water for around a minute. Drain and set aside to cool.
To serve, pour custard into each bowl and top with an 'island'.

Tip • The egg-whites can also be cooked in the microwave. Drop spoonfuls of the mixture directly on the cooking surface one at a time and cook for 5 seconds at maximum power until the islands puff up a little.

Lychee and pitahaya salad

Serves 6–8
Preparation time: 5 minutes

1 can lychees
1 pitahaya, peeled and cubed (see page 97 for a photograph of this fruit, found in exotic fruit sections of some supermarkets. If you can't find this fruit, use 6 passion fruits.)

Put some lychees and a little of their juice into each bowl and add several cubes of pitahaya.
Diced pears and a few drops of lychee- or pear-flavoured liqueur would go well with this dish.

Poached prunes in Amaretto with ice cream and sweetmeats

Serves 6
Preparation and cooking time: 15 minutes
Chilling time: 30 minutes

20 pitted prunes (preferably *pruneaux d'Agen*)
150 ml (¹/₄ pint) almond liqueur (Amaretto)
3 tablespoons dark brown Demerara sugar
1 carton ice cream, fudge or caramel
a few little marzipan sweetmeats to decorate

Poach the prunes for 7–8 minutes in a little water, the liqueur and the sugar, adding more water if they dry out too quickly. Chill for at least 30 minutes before serving.
Serve a scoop of ice cream with a few prunes and sweetmeats on the side.

Poached prunes in Amaretto with ice cream and sweetmeats

red & pink

Pink lemonade
with rose water

Add a drop of rose water essence
to lemonade and decorate with rose-
petals from your garden (unsprayed
ones, of course!)

Kir royal

raspberry liqueur
Champagne
fresh raspberries

Put a raspberry in each glass, add
a drop of raspberry liqueur and fill
up with well-chilled Champagne.

Appetizers

Tasty taramasalata

Funky, party-pink taramasalata is a perfect canapé food. Don't spend time spreading it on bread or making blinis that end up cold and curling. Just prepare a DIY kit for your guests. Serve it in a bowl and line up lots of toast and hot blinis. Put them in a cloth napkin to keep them warm.

Cracking crisps

Bacon crisps and prawn crackers have a lovely pink hue. You can't serve enough of them. Intersperse them with homemade creations.

Basket cases

Mix a few prawns in some mayonnaise with a dollop of tomato ketchup, a splash of lemon juice and a sprinkle of freshly ground pepper and sea salt. Spoon the mixture into small pastry shells and decorate with a few slices of radish.

Steamy moments

Delicious and filling, but a bit tricky to cook. You can cook steamed dumplings in a big bamboo steamer (available for next to nothing in Asian shops). They'll look lovely on the table and you can forget about chopsticks.

Fishy tales

Steam red mullet and place slices on rectangles of bread lightly spread with horseradish, *brandade* (salt cod purée), or smoked mackerel paté. Garnish with a twist of lime.

Pink and peppery

Crush pink peppercorns in butter and spread on slices of white sandwich bread. Voilà!

Charcuterie

Choose the prettiest pink cooked meats and salamis from the many varieties available. You can replenish supplies throughout the evening, but do try to present them nicely. Don't make it look too rough and ready, like a picnic.

Scallop and bacon soup

Haricot bean and pancetta soup

Scallop and bacon soup

This is a very rich soup; a small bowlful per person is quite sufficient

Serves 6
Preparation time: 15 minutes
Cooking time: 15 minutes

2 shallots, finely diced
knob of butter
12–15 scallops, with or without the stalk
400 ml (14 fl oz) whipping cream
6 slices rindless bacon
milk
salt and pepper

Turn the shallots gently in the butter until barely coloured then add the scallops and fry quickly for a few minutes.
Add the cream and heat through blending in the cooking juices. Remove from the heat and set aside.
In another pan, cook the bacon until crisp. Drain well on kitchen paper.
Blend the scallops, shallots, cream and bacon in a liquidizer.
Add milk or cream until the mixture takes on a creamy consistency.
Reheat very gently before serving.

Haricot bean and pancetta soup

Serves 6
Preparation time: 15 minutes
Cooking time: 10 minutes

1 large can haricot beans
500 ml (17 fl oz) vegetable bouillon or stock
8 thin slices pancetta
200 ml (7 fl oz) whipping cream
salt and pepper

Rinse and drain the haricot beans, and put into a large saucepan with the vegetable bouillon.
Grill the pancetta. Add two slices to the beans and simmer for a few minutes.
Blend in a liquidizer, add the cream, season, and decorate each portion with a strip of pancetta.

Tartiflette soup

VERY VERY rich. Imagine tartiflette ground and diluted with cream. A little goes a long way. Excellent for après-ski parties.

Serves 6
Preparation time: 15 minutes
Cooking time: 35 minutes

2 potatoes, peeled
250 ml (8 fl oz) milk
150 g (5 oz) Reblochon cheese
250 ml (8 oz) whipping cream
100 g (3$^1/_2$ oz) lardons or diced streaky bacon

Cook the potatoes in boiling water. When ready, purée them and add enough milk to give a creamy consistency. Add the cheese cut in pieces and heat gently until it melts into the liquid. Pour in the cream.
Brown the lardons and add them to the soup. Season lightly.

Tartiflette soup

Prawn salad with pink grapefruit and chilli mousse

Serves 6
Preparation time: 20 minutes
Cooking time: 5 minutes

20 langoustines, uncooked
3 pink grapefruit
1 egg white
3 tablespoons mayonnaise
2 teaspoons dried chillies, finely ground, (preferably *piment d'Espelette*, if you can find some)
sea salt, freshly milled white pepper

Plunge the langoustines into a large saucepan of boiling, seasoned water and cook for 4–5 minutes. Cool them by plunging into cold water and peel, leaving the tails intact.
Peel the grapefruit and cut into bite-sized pieces.
Whisk the egg white to a peak, add the mayonnaise blended with the chillies. Season to taste.
Assemble the salad ingredients and pour the sauce mousseline over just before serving.

Chicory and feta salad with pomegranate seeds

Serves 6
Preparation time: 5 minutes

3 heads pink chicory
6 heart of lettuce leaves
150 g (5 oz) feta cheese
1 pomegranate

Trim the chicory and lettuce and chop roughly. Dice the feta cheese coarsely, mix into the salad and sprinkle with pomegranate seeds.
Serve with an olive oil and white wine vinegar vinaigrette.

Crab and pink potato salad with horseradish sauce

Serves 6
Cooking time: 20 minutes
Preparation time: 10 minutes

12 small waxy potatoes
1 tablespoon mayonnaise
2 tablespoons whipping cream
2 teaspoons horseradish sauce
250 g (8 oz) cooked crabmeat, (available vacuum-packed)
handful of pink peppercorns
sea salt and freshly milled black pepper

Cook the potatoes, unpeeled, in boiling water. Cool, peel and slice into rounds.
Prepare the sauce by blending the mayonnaise, cream and horseradish.
Just before serving, heat up the potatoes in the microwave or by steaming them, then top with the crabmeat, pour over a little horseradish sauce and sprinkle with pink peppercorns.

Pink coleslaw

Serves 6
Preparation time: 15 minutes

For the salad:
200 g (7 oz) white cabbage, finely chopped
150 g (5 oz) fennel, finely chopped
15 radishes, cut into rounds

For the vinaigrette:
3 tablespoons orange juice
2 tablespoons lime juice
2 tablespoons soy sauce
1 tablespoon sesame oil
2 tablespoons rice vinegar

Make the vinaigrette ahead of time by simply mixing together all the ingredients.
Assemble the salad just before serving and serve the vinaigrette on the side so that people can help themselves.

Poached salmon in Thai bouillon

Serves 10
Preparation time: 20 minutes
Cooking time: 10 minutes

For the Thai seasoning:
50 g (2 oz) fresh root ginger, peeled and finely diced
3 garlic cloves, finely chopped
2 lemon grass stalks, finely chopped
2 shallots, finely diced

For the poached salmon:
3 cans coconut milk
1 litre (1^3/$_4$ pints) fish stock
juice of 5 limes
5–6 tablespoons fish sauce (Nam Pla, Nuoc Mam)
2 tablespoons sesame oil
6–7 salmon fillets, skinned and cut into bite-sized pieces
500 g (1 lb) fragrant Thai rice

Grind the ingredients for the seasoning finely, using a
mini-chopper and blend well together.
Bring to the boil the coconut milk, stock and the Thai
seasoning blend. Cook for several minutes.
Ten minutes before serving, add the lime juice, fish sauce
and sesame oil to the stock and poach the salmon for
5–10 minutes. Serve in bowls with hot rice, cooked according
to instructions on the packet.

Eton mess

Pink trifle with rhubarb and white chocolate

Eton mess (meringue with crushed strawberries)

I'm drawn to dishes with 'mess' in their names. This one is served annually at Eton College prize-giving.

You could present this dish in 'kit' form or as a 'mess'. The pink juice of the strawberries running into the cream and meringue has a pretty effect. Gosh, I'm hungry … If using out-of-season strawberries, give them a boost with a little kirsch.

Serves 6
Preparation time: 15 minutes

250 ml (8 fl oz) whipping cream
2 tablespoons mascarpone cheese (not essential, but it makes the cream particularly creamy)
2–3 tablespoons sugar
500 g (1 lb) strawberries
3–4 tablespoons kirsch if your strawberries are not top-notch
6 meringue shapes (ready-made or your own, if you have time – see recipe below)

Whip the cream until it thickens slightly, adding the mascarpone if desired. Add some sugar. Slice the strawberries, sprinkle with sugar and, if necessary, kirsch. Mix into the cream and, here comes the fun bit, break up the meringues and mix them in too to make a lovely, colourful 'mess'.

Meringues

I know that very sophisticated methods exist for making meringues. Some require three hours' cooling in a cold oven, or whisking in very precise stages. Here is my recipe for stress-free, perfectly respectable meringues.

Makes about 12 meringues
Preparation time: 10 minutes
Cooking time: 50 minutes

5 eggs
250 g (8 oz) caster sugar

Preheat the oven to 120°C (250°F) gas mark ½.
Separate the eggs. Put the whites in a very clean bowl and whisk with an electric beater. When they begin to stiffen, add the sugar, a spoonful at a time, whisking in after every spoonful.
When the meringue is stiff and glossy, drop spoonfuls on a silicone mat or greaseproof paper on top of an ovenproof tray. Cook for around 50 minutes. Remove from the oven and leave to cool on the tray.

Pink trifle with rhubarb and white chocolate

Serves 12–15
Preparation time: 20 minutes
Cooking time: 15 minutes
Chilling time: 2 hours

500 ml (17 fl oz) whipping cream
150 g (5 oz) good white chocolate, broken into small pieces
6 7 rhubarb sticks, peeled and sliced or 250 g (8 oz) frozen rhubarb (less pink, alas).
3–4 tablespoons sugar
1 packet boudoir biscuits

Bring the cream to boiling point and pour it over the white chocolate. Stir until the chocolate has completely melted into the cream. Chill in the refrigerator for 2 hours.
Poach the rhubarb over a low heat in a very little water so that the fruit does not stick to the saucepan. Add sugar, but not too much: the fruit's acidity is necessary to 'cut' the sweet chocolate mousse. The rhubarb should be quite soft.
Whip the cream–chocolate mix until it thickens slightly.
Put a layer of biscuits in a serving dish, add the rhubarb then add a layer of cream. Repeat once or twice depending on the size of your bowl.
Set aside a couple of biscuits and crush them to sprinkle on top of the trifle.
Return to the refrigerator for at least 1 hour to let the flavours mingle and the rhubarb juice soak into the biscuits.

Lychees and coconut, with pink and white sorbets

This ice cream is irresistible, both for its colour and its taste.

Serves 8
Preparation time: 10 minutes

1 tub each of lemon and raspberry sorbet
20 fresh lychees, peeled, or 2 cans, drained
50 g (2 oz) desiccated or flaked coconut
pomegranate seeds (optional)

Put a scoop of sorbet in each bowl, add the lychees and sprinkle with coconut and pomegranate seeds if using.

Lychees and coconut with pink and white sorbets

orange & yellow

Grand Marnier and orange juice

A great classic: sweet and delicious

$^2/_3$ freshly squeezed orange juice
$^1/_3$ Grand Marnier
crushed ice
orange slices

Apricot cocktail

$^1/_3$ apricot juice
$^1/_3$ brandy
$^1/_3$ champagne
brown sugar lumps

Mix together the juice and the brandy.
Add the Champagne and drop a sugar lump
in each glass to make the bubbles rise.

Appetizers

Orange and yellow salad

Serves 6
Preparation time: 15 minutes

2 boneless, skinless chicken breasts
2 carrots
1 yellow pepper
6 dried apricots
1 preserved lemon

For the vinaigrette:
3 tablespoons olive oil
1 tablespoon lemon juice
1 tablespoon orange juice
salt and pepper

Cut the chicken breasts into bite-sized pieces.
Shave the carrots into fine strips.
Slice the pepper into thin strips. Dice the apricots and preserved lemon finely.
Mix together the vinaigrette ingredients.
Mix all the salad ingredients together and hand round the vinaigrette separately.

Here are a few ideas for the 'I'm-not-cooking-but-I'm-fussy-about-my-orange-theme' brigade

Hummus with raisins, oranges and carrots

Preparation time: 15 minutes
Cooking time: 15 minutes

1 x 400 g (14 oz) can chickpeas
3 tablespoons olive oil
grated rind and juice of 1 orange
2 tablespoons tahini
3 carrots, grated
3 tablespoons raisins
salt and pepper

Drain and rinse the chickpeas. Put them in a saucepan, cover with water and simmer for 15 minutes.
Blend in a liquidizer, leave to cool then add the oil, orange juice and rind, tahini and half the carrots and raisins. Season to taste. Transfer to a serving bowl and garnish with the rest of the carrots and raisins. Ideal for dipping or spreading.

Prawns with cocktail sauce

Serves 6
Preparation time: 5 minutes

1 carrot
18–24 cooked, peeled prawns
small bowl of cocktail sauce (you could make it yourself, but readymade will go down just as well, so why bother?)

Peel and slice the carrot in half lengthways to use as a stand for the prawns. Arrange the prawns on top.
Serve the sauce on the side and don't forget a little bowl for the tails.

Salmon carpaccio with pink peppercorns

Serves 6
Preparation time: 5 minutes

150–200 g (5–7 oz) fresh salmon, sliced finely (chill the salmon in the refrigerator or put in the freezer for 30 minutes as this make the fine slicing easier)
3 lemons, quartered
sea salt, pink peppercorns, freshly milled black pepper

Arrange the ingredients prettily and let your guests marinate their own mouthfuls of salmon.

Taramasalata and salmon caviar on black bread

Makes a dozen small slices
Preparation time: 5 minutes

1 pot salmon taramasalata
3–4 slices black bread
1 pot salmon roe

Spread the taramasalata on the bread and top with the salmon roe 'caviar'.

Easy duck with orange

Honey-roast pumpkin with ginger and cumin

Easy duck with orange

My children prefer my way of preparing this classic dish. It reheats very well, which is useful when you are catering for a crowd.

Serves 8
Cooking time: 2 hours
Preparation time: 10 minutes

2 good-sized ducks
grated rind and juice of 3 oranges
3 oranges, peeled and segmented, all pith removed
75 g (3 oz) sugar
50 g (2 oz) butter
150 ml (¼ pint) chicken stock
salt and pepper

Rub the ducks with the grated rind of 1 of the oranges then tuck it into the cavities and put them in a large roasting dish and roast at 190°C (375°F) gas mark 5 for 1¼–1½ hours.
Remove the ducks from the oven and cut the flesh into bite-sized pieces (not like the photograph!) Set aside.
Scrape up the cooking juices and reserve.
Make a caramel by heating the sugar in a heavy-bottomed saucepan. Add the butter then the orange juice and remaining grated rind and the stock. Heat gently until the sugar dissolves anew into the sauce.
Skim off as much fat as possible from the duck cooking juices. Add the juices to the sauce. Bring to the boil and reduce slightly. Season.
Before serving, add the duck and the orange quarters then reheat the whole dish gently.
Serve with firm-fleshed potatoes.

Tip • If you don't have any good chicken stock handy (99% of the time!) you can get commercial stocks that also thicken the sauce. Unfortunately, they have a very strong and salty taste. The ones I prefer can be bought in liquid form, in little cartons in the supermarket.

Roast pumpkin with honey, ginger and cumin

Serves 6
Preparation time: 10 minutes
Cooking time: 40 minutes

800 g (1½ lb) peeled pumpkin
4 tablespoons olive oil
1 tablespoon sugar
1 tablespoon ground cumin
1 thumb-sized piece fresh root ginger, peeled and finely diced
2 tablespoons honey
salt and pepper

Preheat the oven to 180°C (350°F) gas mark 4.
Cut the pumpkin into chunks and place in a roasting dish.
In a bowl, mix together the remaining ingredients then pour them over the pumpkin. Turn well to cover the chunks in the oil-spice-salt-sugar mixture then roast for around 40 minutes.
Serve with good crusty bread, toasted, and crème fraîche.

Spiced squash soup

Serves 6
Preparation time: 10 minutes
Cooking time: 25 minutes

1 kg (2 lb) squash, peeled
500 ml (17 fl oz) water
1 tablespoon ground cinnamon
1 teaspoon ground cloves
whipping cream, to decorate
sea salt and white pepper

Put the squash in a large saucepan with the water.
Bring to the boil then simmer gently for around 25 minutes until quite soft.
Blend in a liquidizer, adding more water if necessary to improve the consistency. Add the spices and season to taste.
Reheat the soup and decorate with a swirl of cream just before serving.

Spiced squash soup

Orange salad with orange-flower syrup

Orange trifle

Orange salad with orange-flower syrup

A classic, always delicious. To be served well-chilled.

Serves 6
Preparation time: 20 minutes
Chilling time: 2 hours

6 good-sized, juicy oranges with thin skins
1 tablespoon orange-flower syrup

Slice 4 unpeeled oranges into thin rounds. Pare the zest from the remaining 2 oranges with a zester, or grate the rind, and squeeze out the juice. Mix zest and juice with the orange-flower syrup.
Chill for at least 2 hours.

Orange trifle

Yet another version of trifle, inspired by Boodle's Club in London.

Serves 8–10
Preparation time: 15 minutes
Refrigeration time: 6 hours

12 sponge fingers (boudoir biscuits)
2 oranges, segmented and cut into pieces
2 tablespoons Grand Marnier liqueur, if desired
500 ml (17 fl oz) whipping cream
75 g (3 oz) sugar
grated rind and juice of 2 oranges
grated rind of 2 lemons, plus 8 tablespoons of juice

Put the sponge fingers in the bottom of a bowl or glass dish. Arrange the orange segments over (reserve a few for decoration) and pour in the Grand Marnier, if using.
Whip the cream lightly then add the sugar, grated rinds, orange juice and as much of the lemon juice as you like. Beat well to incorporate.
Pour over the fruit and leave to chill in the refrigerator for at least 5 hours, to allow the juice to soak well into the sponge fingers.
Decorate with remaining orange segments.

Rice with two apricots and vanilla

Serves 8
Preparation time: 10 minutes
Cooking time: 35 minutes

100 g (3^1/$_2$ oz) sugar
1 litre (1^3/$_4$ pints) milk
3 vanilla pods
300 g (10 oz) pudding rice
20 dried apricots, chopped
12 fresh, ripe apricots, pitted and chopped

Pour half the sugar into the milk and bring to the boil.
Add 2 vanilla pods split lengthways and the rice, then cook, stirring constantly, for around 35 minutes or until all the milk is absorbed and the rice soft.
Add half the dried and fresh apricots. Press the rice into a ring-mould, cover with clingfilm and leave in the refrigerator to chill thoroughly.
Put the remaining dried apricots in a saucepan, barely cover with water and add the rest of the sugar and the third vanilla pod, also split. Simmer to soften the apricots until the water reduces to a syrup. Add the remaining fresh apricots and cook a few minutes longer. The apricots should retain their shape. Chill and serve with the ring of cold rice.

Rice with two apricots and vanilla

green

Appetizers

Petits pois and almond hummus

Serves 6
Cooking time: 10 minutes
Preparation time: 5 minutes

350 g (12 oz) frozen petits pois
1 garlic clove
juice of 2 lemons or more if necessary
4–5 tablespoons olive oil
2–3 tablespoons chopped almonds
2 tablespoons almond paste or tahini
flat leaf parsley, finely chopped
sea salt and black pepper

Cook the petits pois in boiling water until soft.
Purée them in a liquidizer along with the garlic clove.
Add the other ingredients and mix well.
Sprinkle with parsley and serve with flatbread.

Toast with pistachios and almonds

Makes 20 pieces
Preparation time: 5 minutes
Cooking time: 10 minutes

150 g (5 oz) shelled pistachio nuts
75 g (3 oz) almonds, blanched
100 g (3¹/₂ oz) Parmesan cheese
2 tablespoons fresh basil
3 tablespoons olive oil
5 slices white sandwich bread
salt and pepper

Process all the ingredients, except the bread, in a mini-processor. Spread over the bread and toast under the grill for a few minutes. Cut the slices into quarters and serve immediately.

Coconut and cucumber rice rolls

Makes 12 rolls
Cooking time: 15 minutes
Preparation time: 15 minutes

50 g (2 oz) fragrant Thai rice
2–3 tablespoons coconut milk
1 cucumber
fresh coriander
salt and pepper

Cook the rice in boiling water according to the packet instructions. When it is nearly cooked, add the coconut milk and cook further until it is soft. Season and leave to cool.
Carefully slice the cucumber into long, thin strips, using a potato peeler.
Make balls of rice with your fingers and roll the cucumber strips around them.
Secure with a skewer and a coriander leaf.
Serve with satay sauce (available in supermarkets and delicatessen.)

Roast asparagus

When grilled, the little spears of asparagus tips are crunchy and delicious.

Serves 6
Cooking time: 15 minutes
Preparation time: 3 minutes

12 spears green asparagus
2 tablespoons olive oil
sea salt

Preheat the oven to 180°C (350°F) gas mark 4.
Put the asparagus spears in a roasting dish and drizzle with olive oil. Shake the pan to cover them with oil. Roast for 12–15 minutes.
Serve them warm with a light herb mayonnaise or with wasabi, to stick with the green theme. Sprinkle with sea salt.

Mojitos

100 ml (3¹/₂ fl oz) white rum
2 teaspoons sugar
4–5 leaves fresh mint
juice of half a lime
ice cubes
1 slice lime
soda water

Put all the ingredients, except the slice of lime and the
soda water, in a cocktail shaker. Mix well, pour into a
tumbler, add soda water to taste and the slice of lime.

Guacamole soup

Serves 6
Preparation time: 15 minutes
Cooking time: 10 minutes

3 garlic cloves, finely chopped
2 onions, finely diced
oil, for frying
1 litre (1$^3/_4$ pints) vegetable bouillon
grated rind and juice of 3 limes
5 ripe avocados, peeled, stoned and cut into pieces
5 tomatoes, blanched, peeled, deseeded and finely diced
1 bunch fresh coriander, finely chopped
3 corn tortillas
salt and pepper

Cook the garlic and onion in a pan with a little oil until
golden. Add the vegetable bouillon, lime juice and the
avocados. Bring to the boil then remove from the heat and
blend in a liquidizer. Season to taste.
Before serving, reheat gently and add the diced tomatoes,
grated lime rind and the coriander.
Serve with the corn tortillas that have been lightly browned in
a little butter.

Chervil and parsley soup

Serves 6–8
Preparation time: 10 minutes
Cooking time: 20 minutes

1 bunch flat leaf parsley
2 bunches chervil
2 tablespoons olive oil
knob of butter
4 shallots, finely chopped
3 potatoes, peeled and diced
750 ml (1¼ pints) chicken or vegetable bouillon
200 ml (7 fl oz) whipping cream
sea salt and freshly milled black pepper

Strip off the parsley and chervil leaves, reserving a few
chervil leaves for a garnish, and scald briefly, so that they
keep their colour.
Chop the stalks finely and cook gently in the olive oil and
butter, together with the shallots. When they have softened,
add the potatoes and cook for 10 minutes over a gentle heat.
Add the bouillon and cook for a further 15 minutes.
Add the parsley and chervil leaves and cook for another
5 minutes. Finally, stir in the cream and warm through.
Serve piping hot garnished with chervil leaves.

If time permits, make little individual salads or present the ingredients separately so that everyone can make their own.

Grilled courgettes with feta and mint

Serves 6
Preparation time: 5 minutes
Cooking time: 10 minutes

3 medium courgettes or 6 small ones,
sliced thinly lengthways
olive oil
250 g (8 oz) feta cheese, crumbled
a few sprigs of mint
salt and pepper

Dry-fry the courgettes, if possible in a cast-iron ridged griddle pan to give pretty stripes. The slices should be thin enough to cook with a quick flash on the grill, turning once or twice. Sprinkle with olive oil, salt and pepper then add the feta and the mint sprigs.
In the photograph, I have used baby courgettes, increasingly to be found in good supermarkets and vegetable stalls.

Mozzarella, capers and rocket

Serves 6
Preparation time: 5 minutes

150 g (5 oz) mozzarella di bufala (buffalo mozzarella –
no excuses, it's available everywhere)
150 g (5 oz) rocket
3 tablespoons capers
olive oil
salt and freshly milled black pepper

Drain the mozzarella and cut into bite-sized pieces, mix with the rocket, sprinkle with capers, olive oil, salt and pepper.

Fine green beans, steamed mangetout, green olives

Serves 6
Preparation time: 5 minutes
Cooking time: 15 minutes

150 g (5 oz) fine green beans
120 g (4 oz) mangetout
olive oil
white wine vinegar
garlic, chopped very finely
3 tablespoons green olives
salt and pepper

Cook the beans and mangetout briefly in rapid boiling water or by steaming. They should remain very crunchy. Make a vinaigrette with the oil, vinegar, garlic, salt and pepper then stir into the vegetables and add the olives.

Palm hearts, avocado, baby spinach, lime

Serves 6
Preparation time: 10 minutes

1 can palm hearts
2 ripe avocados
juice of 2 limes
100 g (3½ oz) baby spinach
olive oil
salt and pepper

Drain the palm hearts and cut into long strips. Peel the avocados, cut into strips and pour over the juice of 1 lime. Season the spinach shoots with the oil, the remaining lime juice, salt and pepper. Mix with the avocados and arrange on the palm heart strips.

Fillet of cod, wilted spinach, mashed potatoes
and chive sauce

Fillet of cod, wilted spinach, mashed potatoes and chive sauce

This recipe requires two last-minute operations but they are so simple that you will manage easily, even stylishly. For peace of mind, make the mashed potatoes and sauce ahead of time and get the cod fillets ready in the roasting dish.

Serves 8
Cooking time: 30 minutes
Preparation time: 20 minutes

1.5 kg (3 lb) potatoes, peeled and quartered
150 ml ($^1/_4$ pint) whipping cream
125 g (4 oz) butter
1 bunch chives, snipped – reserve 2 tablespoons for the sauce
8 cod fillets, each weighing about 120 g (4 oz)
4 tablespoons lemon juice
400 g (13 oz) fresh spinach leaves, washed and chopped
sea salt, pepper

For the sauce:
2 shallots, finely diced
50 g (2 oz) butter
small glass white wine
500 ml (17 fl oz) whipping cream

2 tablespoons flat leaf parsley, chopped
sea salt, pepper

Cook the potatoes in boiling water until they are quite soft. Mash them with the cream, 50 g (2 oz) butter, salt and pepper. Put to one side.
To make the sauce, cook the shallots gently in a pan with a little of the butter. When they are soft and transparent, add the wine and simmer gently for around 12 minutes to reduce the liquid. Pour in the cream and stir. Set aside.
Put the cod fillets in a large roasting dish. Pour over the lemon juice and put a small knob of butter on each fillet. Season lightly. Preheat the oven to 220°C (425°F) Gas Mark 7 and roast for 5–6 minutes. The fish should remain soft and almost transparent.
Meanwhile, heat some olive oil in a pan and rapidly stir-fry the spinach leaves until wilted. Drain well and season to taste.
Reheat the mashed potatoes and add the snipped chives.
Reheat the sauce and add the remaining butter, whipping lightly to thicken the sauce. Add the 2 tablespoons snipped chives and season.
To serve, put a spoonful of spinach on each plate, add a dollop of mash, mixed with chives, and a cod fillet. Pour the sauce over and serve immediately.

Green chicken curry

If you are short of time, buy a ready-made good all-purpose green Thai curry sauce.

Serves 6–8
Preparation time: 15 minutes
Cooking time: 25 minutes

For the green Thai curry paste:
2 lemon grass stalks, chopped
5 green peppers, deseeded and finely chopped
2 shallots, chopped
25 g (1 oz) fresh root ginger, peeled and finely chopped
3 garlic cloves
1 bunch fresh coriander
2 teaspoons ground cumin
1 teaspoon ground coriander
2 tablespoons fish sauce (Nam Pla, Nuoc Mam)

500 ml (17 fl oz) coconut milk
300 ml ($^1/_2$ pint) chicken bouillon
2 tablespoons soy sauce
1 tablespoon sesame oil
2 tablespoons fish sauce
500 g (1 lb) boneless, skinless chicken breasts, cooked and sliced into fine strips
1 bunch basil, chopped
1 bunch fresh coriander, chopped

Make the curry paste by blending all the ingredients in a mini-processor.
Put the paste in a saucepan and cook gently for 3–4 minutes, stirring. Add the coconut milk and simmer for 10 minutes then add the bouillon, soy sauce, sesame oil, fish sauce and the chicken breasts.
Simmer for a further 10 minutes.
Serve with fragrant Thai rice sprinkled with chopped fresh herbs.

Green chicken curry

Spring vegetable pesto

Serves 6
Cooking time: 15 minutes
Preparation time: 15 minutes

6 good-sized green asparagus spears
100 g (3$^1/_2$ oz) petits pois
100 g (3$^1/_2$ oz) shelled broad beans
150 g (5 oz) Parmesan cheese, grated
3–4 tablespoons olive oil
small bunch of basil
2 tablespoons lemon juice
salt and pepper

Steam or boil the vegetables until they are quite soft.
Cut off the asparagus tips and set aside with a few petits pois
and some beans.
Process the remaining vegetables with the Parmesan cheese,
olive oil, basil, lemon juice, salt and pepper until it forms
a thick paste. Add the reserved asparagus tips, petits pois
and beans.
Serve with hot pasta.

Pistachio mousse

Serves 8
Preparation time: 15 minutes

250 g (8 oz) whipping cream
150 g (5 oz) caster sugar
150 g (5 oz) pistachio nuts
1 tablespoonful Amaretto (almond liqueur)
a few drops of natural pistachio or almond essence

Whip the cream lightly with the sugar.
Grind the pistachio nuts into a paste and add the whipped cream, Amaretto and essence.
Serve in small bowls or glasses with brandy snaps.

Minty kiwi and cinnamon salad

Serves 6
Preparation time: 15 minutes
Cooking time: 10 minutes

150 g (5 oz) sugar
300 ml (1/2 pint) water
1 cinnamon stick
12 kiwifruit, peeled and sliced into rounds
few sprigs of fresh mint

Put the sugar, water and cinnamon stick in a saucepan and simmer gently until the sugar dissolves. Cook for 10 minutes until it turns syrupy. Allow to cool, then remove the cinnamon. Pour over the kiwifruit and add a sprig of mint to each glass. Serve well chilled.

A celebration lunch

Baptisms, communions, weddings . . .

. . . engagements, Christmas festivities and Easter lunches, we all need to get together from time to time. When the party is being held at your place, if you are short of experience or inspiration, without access to a caterer, anti-depressants or your cordon bleu friends, it can sometimes take on dramatic proportions. And even when the members of your family get on together as if they were an advertisement for Calvin Klein's 'Eternity', you tend to feel 'on-stage', at the mercy of great-aunt Gertrude's inevitable comments. It's difficult to please so many generations and – above all – not to spend 5 hours at table on the first fine weekend of the year.

A FEW WORDS OF ADVICE

1 Prepare everything, absolutely everything, in advance. Obviously, this means devoting at least the previous evening to it.

2 Tailor the menu according to whether you will be seated or standing. This makes a difference.

3 Break the ice with your aperitifs but not your back or the bank with your dishes.

4 Serve meat or fish as simply as possible, then go to town on the accompaniments. Everyone can tuck in to what they like and even little Miss Picky (your nephew's vegetarian girlfriend) and James (your brother's 8-month-old son) can feast to their heart's content.

5 A really stylish dessert is indispensable. Nothing marks a traditional celebration better than a superb centrepiece (see page 7).

My advice would be to get a professional caterer, or a patisserie, to provide a magnificent finale, given that you will have spent less on the other courses. You can simply accompany it with a fresh fruit salad.

Open sandwiches: foie gras, dried apricots and pepper;
bacon and melon; bacon and oranges; pecorino cheese and chutney

Nectarine and chorizo sausage open sandwich

Appetizers

Assorted open sandwiches

Let your imagination run riot. Open sandwiches can be varied
ad infinitum and feed the hungry without too much work.
Here are several sweet–savoury combinations.

Foie gras, dried apricots and pepper
Bacon and melon
Pecorino cheese and chutney
Bacon and oranges
Nectarine and chorizo sausage
Cabbage, chestnuts and smoked salmon

Vegetables make great readymade, edible bases. Go for it.

Endives with camembert and cranberries

Poach a few cranberries in water. Add a little sugar at the end
to reduce their acidity. Fill endive leaves with a bit of
Camembert and a few poached cranberries.

Baby peppers stuffed with salt cod purée (*brandade*) or fish paté

If you can find them, baby peppers make delightful multi-
colourful containers.

Potatoes with horseradish and smoked eel

Boil or steam the potatoes. Cut in half, spread with
horseradish and top with a strip of smoked eel.

Crackers, oatcakes and pastry shells

Some you can buy, others will be homemade. Don't hesitate
to combine readymade products with those you've prepared
yourself. You'll be adding a personal touch with your choice
of combinations. Here are a few ideas:

Oatcakes or crackers with Parmesan and:
Quince jelly
Bacon and dried pineapple
Mozzarella and balsamic vinegar

Pastry shells with:
Tomatoes, strawberries, balsamic vinegar
Roast beef, sweet Thai chilli sauce

Oatcakes with Parmesan and quince jelly

Endives with camembert and cranberries

Potatoes with horseradish and smoked eel

Cabbage, chestnuts and smoked salmon open sandwich

Baby peppers stuffed with *brandade* or fish paté

Pastry shells

Prune and apple casserole with honey

Roast duck breasts

Roast duck with prune and apple casserole

Serves 12
Preparation time: 15 minutes
Cooking time: 45–50 minutes

6 duck breasts (i.e. from 3 whole duck)
12 confit of duck thighs (see right-hand column
for cooking instructions)
6 apples, peeled and quartered (Cox's orange pippin,
Braeburn, French origin Boskoop)
12 prunes, pitted and quartered
4 tablespoons runny honey
knob of butter
salt and pepper

Preheat the oven to 180°C (350°F) gas mark 4.
Take the duck pieces from the refrigerator 30 minutes before
cooking. Put the duck breasts in a roasting dish and cook for
40–50 minutes. Test with a sharp skewer.
Put the apples, prunes, honey and butter in an ovenproof
dish. Season, cover and put in the oven 30 minutes before
the duck has finished roasting.
Rest the meat for 10 minutes before carving.

Shallot mash

Serves 12

100 g (3$\frac{1}{2}$ oz) butter
6 shallots, finely chopped
10 floury potatoes, peeled and quartered
200 ml (7 fl oz) whipping cream
salt and pepper

Put 25 g (1 oz) of the butter in a small saucepan and cook
the shallots until golden.
Cook the potatoes in boiling salted water. Drain and mash
well, incorporating the cream and the remaining butter.
Adjust the seasoning and add the shallots.

Confit of duck thighs

*(Confit of duck thighs is a French speciality which can be
found in Britain although you may have to use a mail-order
speciality food supplier, unless you have a super delicatessen
near by.)*

The objective is to combine the textures of the roast and
confit. That way you'll double your chance of pleasing
everyone!

I buy my confits! I've made confit of duck once in my life.
We had great fun on our little farm but I spent three days
at it, until I felt almost preserved myself.

Heat the duck thighs to reduce the fat then reheat again
in the oven just before serving, to give a crunchy finish.

Confit of duck thighs

Vegetable gratin + shallot mash

'Traditional' roast leg of lamb

'Traditional' roast leg of lamb

Serves 8–10
Preparation time: 3 minutes
Cooking time: approximately 1¹/₂ hours

1 leg of lamb weighing approximately 2 kg (4 lb)
5 garlic cloves, peeled and sliced
large sprig rosemary, leaves stripped and finely chopped
2–3 tablespoons olive oil

Take the lamb from the refrigerator half an hour before cooking. Preheat the oven to 220°C (425°F) gas mark 7.
Mix the garlic and rosemary leaves with the olive oil.
Score the meat all over and insert the garlic slices.
Rub in the olive oil and rosemary.
Cook for half an hour then lower the temperature to 180°C (350°F) gas mark 4 and cook for another hour. The meat can be covered midway through the cooking to ensure that it is cooked through, but some like it quite pink. Check with a sharp skewer.

Slow-cooked leg of lamb

Serves 8–10
Preparation time: 3 minutes
Cooking time: 6 hours (at least!)

1 leg of lamb weighing approximately 2 kg (4 lb)
5 garlic cloves, peeled and sliced
large sprig rosemary, leaves stripped and finely chopped
2–3 tablespoons olive oil

Take the lamb from the refrigerator half an hour before cooking. Preheat the oven to 110°C (225°F) gas mark ¹/₄.
Prepare the lamb as above and put in the oven. Baste it and cover halfway through cooking time, especially if you are using a fan oven. Don't worry about 'forgetting' it and leaving it to slow-cook. This is a perfect recipe if you have to attend a ceremony before lunch – if you have a cool head, that is. It's what I like to do, although others may prefer to watch over it.

Vegetable gratin

Serves 8–10
Preparation time: 15 minutes
Cooking time: 45 minutes for the 'traditional' roast;
2 hours for the slow-cooked lamb

2 aubergines
4 courgettes
4 tomatoes
3 onions
olive oil
4 garlic cloves, crushed
thyme, finely chopped
rosemary, finely chopped
salt and pepper

Slice the vegetables into thin rounds. Layer them in an ovenproof dish, with a little seasoning between each layer, alternating the colours. Drizzle with plenty of olive oil and sprinkle with garlic, thyme and rosemary. Cook alongside the 'traditional' roast for 45–50 minutes. If you are serving with the slow-cooked lamb, it's best to cover the vegetables with cooking foil or to use a covered dish and cook for 2 hours.

Roast poussin and triple-citrus mash

This is a very good way to avoid the problem of making sure everyone has a choice of white or brown meat. With a whole poussin everyone gets thighs, breast, or what-they-will. There's no need for anyone to feel hard done by!

Serves 12
Preparation time: 20 minutes
Cooking time: 1¹/₂ hours

6 poussins
2 garlic cloves, peeled
pared rind of 1 lemon and 1 lime (no pith!)
3 tablespoons olive oil
15 potatoes peeled and diced
150 ml (¹/₄ pint) milk
150 ml (¹/₄ pint) whipping cream
grated rind of 3 lemons and 2 limes
1 preserved lemon, finely diced
sea salt and freshly milled black pepper

Preheat the oven to 190°C (375°F) gas mark 5.
Rub the poussins with garlic. Tuck the pared rind from 1 lemon and 1 lime inside the you-know-where of each bird (the cavity, if you are still wondering) and season, drizzle with olive oil and cook for 1–1¹/₂ hours, depending on your oven's efficiency. Baste from time to time.
Cook the potatoes until soft. Mash with the milk and cream, season with sea salt and pepper. Add the diced preserved lemon and the remaining zests and blend well.
Remove the poussins from the oven and deglaze the roasting-dish with a little water, skim off the fat and reserve the juice.
Serve on a bed of the mashed potatoes and pour over the cooking juices.

Coquelets à rôtir

Carrot and parsnip mash

Rolled and tied veal roast

Roast veal with kidneys and carrot and parsnip mash

Two different textures of meat, simply prepared for everyone to enjoy.

Serves 8
Cooking time: 3 hours

2 tablespoons olive oil
1.5 kg (3 lb) veal fillet, rolled and tied
1 veal kidney, prepared by your butcher
salt and pepper

Preheat the oven to 150°C (300°F) gas mark 2.
Heat the oil in a roasting-tin and brown the veal fillet on all sides. Season lightly then roast for around 2½ hours, basting regularly. If it looks like drying out cover with cooking foil. About 35 minutes before serving, turn the oven up to 200°C (400°F) gas mark 6, sprinkle the kidney with olive oil and roast whole. (If the veal shows that it is ready during this 35 minutes, take it from the oven, cover with kitchen foil and keep warm.) Season and serve with the roast, with carrot and parsnip mash (see p. 168) on the side.

Veal kidney,
prepared by a butcher

Everyone loves hash. The following recipes are all precooked (and even minced, which will please those who don't yet have teeth and also those who have dentures). Everything heats up well and can be eaten with a fork.

Preserved duck with girolles

Serves 8
Preparation time: 25 minutes
Cooking time: 25 minutes (plus reheating time for the duck thighs and purée)

6 confit of duck thighs (see page 158)
300 g (10 oz) girolles or other wild mushrooms
3 shallots, finely chopped

For the purée:
12 potatoes, peeled and quartered
knob of butter, milk, cream, salt and pepper

Heat the duck thighs gently to release their fat.
Remove the flesh and chop into bite-sized pieces.
To make the purée: cook the potatoes and purée with the butter, milk, cream and seasoning.
Lightly brown the mushrooms and shallots and set aside.
To make the hash: cover the duck with the potato purée and top with the mushroom–shallot mixture.
If you want to reheat it, the duck and the potatoes can be prepared in advance but the mushrooms should be cooked at the last minute.

Vegetable hash and mash

It's up to you which vegetables you use, depending on the season, the shape and size of your dishes, the number of guests and … anything you like. Carrots and parsnips go well together, for example (see p. 164). Peel, chop and cook the vegetables until tender and mash roughly. Add a knob of butter and a dollop of cream and mix well together.

Braised veal with orange carrots

Serves 8
Preparation time: 25 minutes
Cooking time: 1 1/2 hours

1 veal fillet
2 carrots, peeled and sliced into rounds
2 onions, finely chopped
2 glasses white wine
salt and pepper

For the orange carrots:
12 carrots, peeled and cut in chunks
olive oil
2 oranges, quartered and sliced
salt

For the purée:
12 potatoes, peeled and quartered
milk, butter, cream
salt and pepper

Preheat the oven to 180°C (350°F) gas mark 4. Brown the meat in a roasting tin, add the 2 carrots cut in rounds and the chopped onions then pour over the wine. Season lightly and roast for around 1 1/2 hours.
To make the orange carrots: put the carrot chunks in an ovenproof dish, sprinkle with olive oil and a pinch of salt. Roast alongside the meat for the last 40 minutes of cooking time. Remove from the oven and stir in the oranges.
Boil the potatoes and purée with milk, butter and cream.
Chop the cooked veal together with the onion and carrots cooked with it, and stir in some of the cooking juices.
Spread a layer of potatoes on top of the hashed meat and top with the carrot–orange mixture.

Shoulder of lamb with chutney

Serves 8
Preparation time: 35 minutes
Cooking time: 2 hours

1 shoulder of lamb
12 floury potatoes, peeled and quartered
butter, whole milk, cream for the purée (optional)
salt and pepper

For the chutney:
2 handfuls of dried fruits cut in two (prunes, pears, figs)
2 teaspoons quatre-épices
1 tablespoon soft brown sugar
2 apples (preferably French Boskoops, or Cox's orange pippins etc.), peeled and chopped
2 pears (Comice), peeled and chopped
2 handfuls of sultanas

Roast the lamb, take off all the meat and chop finely.
Cook the potatoes and purée with milk, butter, salt and pepper.
Poach the dried fruits for 5 minutes in a little water with the spices and sugar. Add the fresh fruit and sultanas and poach for around 5 minutes, until the water evaporates leaving a soft chutney. Fill a dish or a mould with alternating layers of lamb, puréed potatoes and chutney.

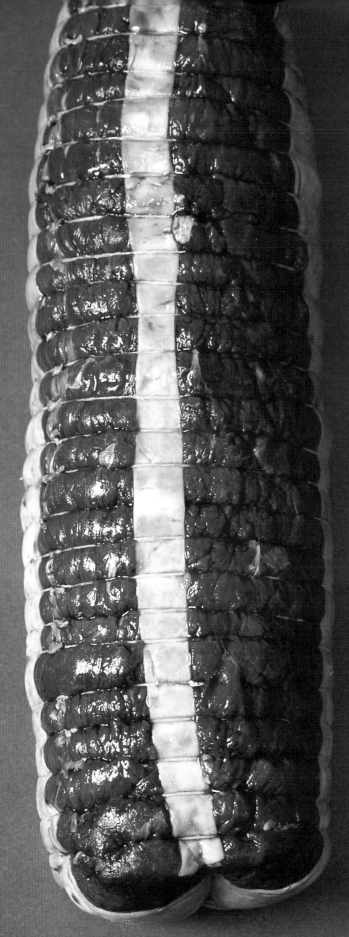

Roast venison

Honey-roast winter vegetables

Roast venison with honey-roast winter vegetables

This makes a great change from the eternal roast: the delicate, unmarinated flavour will please everyone, small and large. Moreover, your butcher does all the work, but give him some notice.

Serves 10
Cooking time: 45 minutes
Preparation time: 15 minutes

3 tablespoons olive oil
3 tablespoons runny honey
12 carrots and/or parsnips, peeled and sliced
(see photo, p.171)
1 head celeriac, peeled and sliced
fillet of venison, approximately 2 kg (4 lb), lovingly
prepared by your butcher
salt and pepper

Preheat the oven to 190°C (375°F) gas mark 5.
Blend the oil and honey and roll the vegetables in the mixture. Roast for 40–45 minutes. Take from the oven and set aside. Forty minutes before serving the meat, preheat the oven to 220–230°C (425–450°F) gas mark 7–8. Roast the venison as for beef for 30–35 minutes until it is well done. Towards the end of the cooking time, reheat the vegetables for a few minutes alongside the meat, then season and serve together.

Quick-roasted salmon fillets, with caper and lemon sauce and smoked salmon

Serves 12
Preparation time: 10 minutes
Cooking time: 10 minutes

12 salmon fillets, with or without skin
500 ml (17 fl oz) whipping cream
3 small jars capers, rinsed and drained
3–4 tablespoons olive oil
2 lemons (to baste the salmon before cooking)
250 g (8 oz) smoked salmon, diced
24 small potatoes, peeled, steamed or boiled
3 lemons, quartered (to garnish)
salt and pepper

Remove the salmon fillets from the refrigerator 15 minutes before cooking.
Make the sauce by seasoning the cream and heating it with the capers. Take care not to season overmuch. You will shortly be adding the diced smoked salmon, which can be salty.
Preheat the oven to 180°C (350°F) gas mark 4.
Put the salmon fillets in an ovenproof dish. Drizzle with a little olive oil and lemon juice. Season. Cook for barely 5 minutes: the centre of the fish should remain moist.
Add the diced smoked salmon to the sauce just before serving, so that it will stay soft.
Serve with the steamed potatoes and garnish with lemon quarters.

There's nothing easier than ordering pre-cooked beef or roasted chicken from your butcher or delicatessen. If you prefer to cook them yourself, here are some recipes to follow.

Roast beef

Serves 8–10
Preparation time: 3 minutes
Cooking time: 1¹/₂ hours

2 kg (4 lb) beef for roasting
olive oil
2 onions, quartered
2 garlic cloves, crushed
salt and finely milled black pepper

Remove the roast from the refrigerator 30 minutes before cooking.
Preheat the oven to 220°C (425°F) gas mark 7.
Heat the olive oil in a roasting tin and quickly seal the meat on all surfaces. Add the onions and garlic and put in the oven.
Cook for 1–1¹/₂ hours. In theory, for rare roast beef, allow 25 minutes per kilo (2 lb), plus 15 minutes. In practice, everything depends on your oven. Just keep testing with a sharp skewer, unless you have a meat thermometer.
Leave the meat to rest and cool completely before carving into thin slices.

Roast chicken

Serves 6–8
Preparation time: 3 minutes
Cooking time: 1¹/₄ hours

1 chicken, weighing 1.5 kg (3 lb)
2 garlic cloves
olive oil
salt

Remove the chicken from the refrigerator 30 minutes before cooking time.
Preheat the oven to 220°C (425°F) gas mark 7.
Rub the skin of the chicken with the garlic, olive oil and salt. Put a clove of garlic and a little salt inside. Put in the oven and cook for around 1 hour. Baste from time to time.
When the chicken has browned nicely, remove from the oven and test by sticking a sharp skewer into the joint between thigh and body. If the juice runs clear, it's done!

Poached salmon

Served 10
Preparation time: 3 minutes
Cooking time: 30 minutes
Chilling time: 2 hours

1 fish-kettle

1 salmon, weighing around 2 kg (4 lb)
¹/₂ bottle white wine
1 onion, peeled and sliced
1–2 carrots, sliced
1 celery stalk, chopped
thyme
bay leaf
salt and pepper

Put the salmon in the fish-kettle, add the wine, vegetables, herbs and seasonings. Add sufficient water just to cover the salmon.
Bring gently to the boil. When the water bubbles, turn off the heat and leave the fish to cool until you can test with your fingers.
Remove the salmon, chill it and carefully remove the skin.

Poached salmon

Caesar salad, French-style

Serves 6–8
Preparation time: 15 minutes
Cooking time: 5 minutes

1 baguette
2 garlic cloves, peeled
4 anchovy fillets, finely sliced
4 tablespoons lemon juice
4–5 tablespoons olive oil
4 hearts of Cos lettuce, washed, dried and leaves separated
3 hard-boiled eggs, quartered lengthways
100 g (3 1/2 oz) Parmesan cheese, grated
salt and pepper

Preheat the oven to 180°C (350°F) gas mark 4. Rub the baguette with one of the garlic cloves and cut into croûton cubes. Drizzle a little olive oil over them to coat and bake until golden brown. Set aside.
Crush the remaining garlic and mix with the anchovy strips, lemon juice and olive oil to make a vinaigrette. Season to taste. Put the lettuce in a serving bowl and pour over the vinaigrette. Mix well to coat the lettuce leaves. Serve garnished with quartered eggs, Parmesan and croûtons.

TMB

Tomato, mozzarella and basil: this poor salad has been badly served over the past few years, like tiramisu and carpaccio of beef with pesto. Some restaurants seem unable to make a good job of presenting Italian dishes with their delicious combinations of flavours. Nowadays you can buy tomatoes with real taste, mozzarella di bufala and wonderfully aromatic fresh herbs. Forget rubbery white cheese, frozen basil and watery tomatoes: this is the real thing, the true taste of Calabria.

Serves 6
Preparation time: 10 minutes

3 balls mozzarella di bufala (buffalo mozzarella),
roughly chopped
6 ripe tomatoes, sliced
olive oil
3–4 sprigs basil
sea salt and freshly ground black pepper

Sprinkle the mozzarella over the tomatoes and drizzle with the olive oil. Tear the basil leaves with your hands and scatter over the salad. Season and serve.

Thai cucumber salad

Serves 6
Preparation time: 10 minutes

300 ml (1/2 pint) white vinegar
150 g (5 oz) sugar
2 cucumbers peeled, deseeded and sliced
2 shallots, finely chopped
35 g (1 1/2 oz) fresh root ginger, peeled and finely diced

Mix the vinegar and sugar until the latter has completely dissolved. Add the remaining ingredients. Serve well chilled.

Beetroot, apples and celery

When I was a child, we had this salad every Sunday evening. It goes down well with cold roast beef.

Serves 6
Preparation time: 10 minutes

2 beetroot, cooked and diced
2 Granny Smith apples, peeled and diced
2 celery sticks, diced
1 tablespoon chopped parsley
salt and pepper

Mix all the ingredients together and serve well chilled.

Goats' cheese with herb 'coulis'

Search out the freshest possible goats' cheeses and serve them whole or sliced in rounds, accompanied with cream cheese blended with whipping cream, a little olive oil and finely chopped fresh herbs (dill, chives, basil, mint, tarragon).

Roast goats' cheese on a brioche, with apple, cranberry and almond compote

This is a pleasing little variation on the cheese course that saves having to hand round a big platter.

Serves 6
Preparation time: 10 minutes
Cooking time: 10 minutes

120 g (4 oz) fresh cranberries
2 Granny Smith apples, peeled and diced
1 tablespoon sugar
2 tablespoons sliced almonds, toasted
6 slices of brioche
3 crottins de Chavignol or other small goats' cheese

Put the cranberries in a pan with a little water and the apples. Poach for 5–7 minutes until the apples begin to soften without losing their shape. Leave to cool, then add a little sugar – to cut the sharpness of the cranberries – and the toasted almonds.
Preheat the oven to 180°C (350°F) gas mark 4.
Toast the brioche slices and stamp out rounds with a pastry-cutter. Cut the cheeses in half and put them in an ovenproof dish. Roast for 2 minutes, remove, place one half on each brioche round and serve with the compote.

Cheese layer-cake

This is a new version of the popular cheese terrine from my previous book *Food For Friends* – but with no butter.

Serves 12
Preparation and assembly time: 30 minutes

1 ripe Camembert cheese
1 large tub mascarpone cheese
75 g (3 oz) raisins
100 g (3½ oz) Gorgonzola cheese
2 tablespoons poppy seeds
1 small carton Saint-Moret cheese (or fresh, soft goats' cheese)
1 white sandwich loaf, thinly sliced and crusts removed
sea salt and freshly milled black pepper

Mix the Camembert and half the mascarpone with a fork until well blended. Add the raisins and season to taste. Set aside. Blend the remaining mascarpone with the Gorgonzola and add the poppy seeds.
Work some black pepper into the Saint-Moret or goats' cheese. Add salt if desired.
Stack the layer-cake, spreading alternating cheeses on the bread, with the goats' cheese in the middle and on top. Neaten the sides. Chill in the refrigerator and serve accompanied by dried fruits and a few sprigs of rocket.

Camembert and caramelized apples

Very, very filling. Eat in moderation.

Serves 6
Preparation time: 10 minutes
Cooking time: 10 minutes

1 ripe Camembert cheese
100 g (3½ oz) sugar
50 g (2 oz) butter
2 tablespoons whipping cream
1 Granny Smith apple, peeled and cut into cubes

Slice the top off the Camembert and carefully scrape out the cheese, being careful not to pierce the rind. This operation is possible only if the cheese is well ripened. Set the rind aside. Make a butter caramel by melting the sugar in a heavy-bottomed saucepan, adding the butter and cream away from the heat when the sugar has carmelized to a golden-brown. If the mixture sticks a bit, reheat it very gently and it will soften. Blend the apple, cheese and caramel together and fill the Camembert rind with the mixture. Serve warm or cold with good hazelnut or walnut bread.

Tip • It doesn't take a Nobel Prize for Physics to work out that not everything will fit back inside the empty Camembert rind once you've mixed the caramel and apples with the cheese. You will also realize that it's best to try out the recipes before inflicting them on your guests. Therefore …

Strawberries, redcurrants and raspberries with raspberry sauce

This recipe depends upon the luck of the draw at your green-grocer's. Blackberries and blueberries are more difficult to find but they would go very well in this pretty fruit salad.

Serves 6
Preparation time: 20 minutes
Cooking time: 5 minutes

500 g (1 lb) strawberries, washed, hulled and sliced
200 g (7 oz) redcurrants, stripped and trimmed
500 g (1 lb) raspberries
2–3 tablespoons sugar

Mix the strawberries and redcurrants with half the raspberries. Put the remaining raspberries and the sugar in a saucepan and cook gently for several minutes to make a *coulis*. Strain this if you want to remove the raspberry seeds. Set aside to cool. Just before serving, pour the *coulis* over the other fruit and stir well.
Serve with vanilla-flavoured mascarpone cheese, brandy snaps or other crunchy little biscuits and, perhaps, red-fruit sorbets.

Papaya and mango salad with orange juice and coconut snowballs

If you can't find coconut balls in the sweetshop and haven't time to make your own, just sprinkle over some desiccated or flaked coconut instead.

Serves 6
Preparation time: 25 minutes

2 ripe papayas
3 ripe mangoes
juice of 3 oranges
2–3 passion fruits (optional)
12 little coconut balls

Peel the papayas and mangoes and cut the flesh into small dice. This is a bit fiddly but gives a very pretty effect. If you simply do not have the time, cut the fruits into long strips. Mix with the orange juice. If available, add the juice and seeds of 2 or 3 passion fruit to the orange juice.
Serve with the coconut balls.

Chocolate biscuit cake

Serves 10
Preparation time: 25 minutes
Chilling time: overnight

150 g (5 oz) butter, softened (I really like salted butter
for this cake, but suit yourself)
300 g (10 oz) icing sugar
3 tablespoons cocoa powder blended in a little water
2 packets small very dark chocolate-topped biscuits
(Lu or Choco Leibnitz)
2–3 coffee-cupfuls very strong black coffee

Blend together the butter, icing sugar and cocoa powder.
Soak the underside of each biscuit in the coffee for a few
seconds and arrange in a serving dish, making sure the biscuits
are pressed up close to one another. Carefully spread a layer
of buttercream over. Repeat the operation and top with a final
layer of biscuits.
Leave chilling in the refrigerator overnight if possible.

Triple choc-chip tartlets

Note • a flexible mould is essential for this dish. You can find these in catering specialists, kitchen shops and sometimes in large department stores – mail order too.

Makes 6 tartlets
Preparation time: 30 minutes
Chilling time: 3 hours

2 packets Triple Choc-Chip cookies
70 g (3 oz) salted butter
250 g (8 oz) whipping cream
250 g (8 oz) very dark chocolate (70% chocolate solids), broken into small pieces

Put the cookies in a large bowl and crush finely. Melt the butter and stir it into the cookies. Press the mixture into the cups of a flexible tart-mould around 7–8 cm (3–3$^1/_2$ inches) in diameter. Chill in the refrigerator.
Bring the cream to just boiling point and pour over the broken chocolate. Stir until it takes on a creamy, shiny consistency. Pour over the chilled cookie mixture and return to the refrigerator for several hours, until the chocolate cream firms up.
Unmould and serve.

Acknowledgements

Shopping and table decoration: Pauline Ricard-André

Cardboard plates
Tutti Fiesta – p.12, p.17, p.27

Tableware
Le Bon Marché Rive Gauche – p.45 (knife), p.83, p.125, p.127, p.179
Léonardo – p.102
Siècle – p.179 (mouse)
Tsé-Tsé – p.110, p.119
Tutti Fiesta – p. 97 (plastic cutlery)

Plates and dishes
Asa – p.120, p.129 (green plates), p.129, p.131, p.137, p.142, p.144
Astier de Villatte – p.73 (dishes), p.76 (plates), p.79, pp.80 and 81 (plates), p.87, p.92, p.177 (fantasy plate)
Le Bon Marché Rive Gauche – p.18, p.49, p.58 (salad bowl), p.61 (bowl), p.107, p.135, p.159, p.169 (plates), p.173, p.177, p.179 (plate, bottom left), p.185
Haviland – p.35 (by Françoise Bauchet), p.42, p.129, p.131.
Luneville – p.85
Tsé-Tsé – p.55 (gratin dish), p.89, p.91, p.110, p.139 (shallow bowls), p.140 (plate)

Bowls and serving-dishes
Asa – p.115 (square dish)
Astier de Villate – p.81
Le Bon Marché Rive Gauche – p.49, p.83, p.107
Haviland – p.39, p.51, p.119, p.123
Léonardo – p.84, p.93
Tsé-Tsé – p.22, p.23, p.25, p.27 (bowl)

Cloths, napkins, tablemats, tartans
Cath Kidston – p.37, p.41, p.42, p.45, p.47, p.48
Séquana – p.34

Glassware
Le Bon Marché Rive Gauche – p.133, p.177
Léonardo – p.57 (bowl), p.97 (glass)
Séquana – p.183

Trays
Tsé-Tsé – p.66, p.121, p.127

Useful addresses

ASA
(available in large department stores and specialist shops)
Tel: (0049) 26 24 189 45
Astier de Villatte
173 Rue St Honoré 75001 Paris • Tel: 01 42 60 74 13
Cath Kidston
www.cathkidston.co.uk • Tel: 0207 221 4248
Haviland
25 Rue Royale 75008 Paris • Tel: (0033) 1 42 66 36 36
IKEA
www.IKEA.co.uk
Ladurée
16 Rue Royale 75008 Paris • Tel: (0033) 1 42 60 21 79
www.laduree.fr
Le Bon Marché
24 Rue de Sèvres 75007 Paris • Tel: (0033) 1 44 39 80 00

Léonardo
(sold in major department stores)
Tel: (0033) 3 88 56 85 40
Luneville
30 Rue Chabrol 75010 Paris • Tel: (0033) 1 47 70 57 53
Séquana
64 Av. de La Motte Picquet 75015 Paris •
Tel: (0033) 1 45 66 58 40
Siècle
24 Rue du Bac 75007 Paris • Tel: (0033) 1 47 03 48 03
Tsé-Tsé
Galerie Sentou – 24 Rue du Pont Louis Philippe 75004 Paris •
Tel: (0033) 1 42 71 00 01
Tutti Fiesta
32 Rue des Vignoles 75020 Paris • Tel: (0033) 1 43 70 21 00
www.tuttifiesta.com

For Sophie and Nicolas, remember 2000

Thanks to

– the tough nut, for the evening of flying saucers;
– Catherine and Florence for their valuable input;
– Veronique, for the sweets. Amazing; there are some left!
– Jacqueline, dinette-queen;
– La Maison Ladurée for the magnificent showpiece on page 7;
– Eddie Barclay. Nobody does it better.

And above all, to Thierry, Coco, Tim, Tanguy and Victoire.
Look, I'm here!

Txx

© Marabout (Hachette Livre) 2003
This edition published in 2004 by Hachette Illustrated UK, Octopus Publishing Group Ltd., 2–4 Heron Quays, London E14 4JP

Text and recipes © Trish Deseine
Photographs © Marie-Pierre Morel
Proof-reading, copy-editing: Véronique Dussidour and Antoine Pinchot
English translation by JMS Books LLP
(email: moseleystrachan@blueyonder.co.uk)
Translation © Octopus Publishing Group Ltd.

A CIP catalogue for this book is available from the British Library

ISBN: 1 84430 078 1

Printed in Singapore by Tien Wah Press

Index